See Chapter XXII

SPRINGTIME

THE MAN
IN LONELY LAND

BY

KATE LANGLEY BOSHER

AUTHOR OF

"MARY CARY" "MISS GIBBIE GAULT"

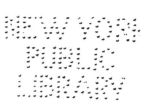

HARPER & BROTHERS PUBLISHERS
NEW YORK AND LONDON
MCMXII

COPYRIGHT, 1912, BY HARPER & BROTHERS
PRINTED IN THE UNITED STATES OF AMERICA
PUBLISHED APRIL, 1912

TO MY BROTHER
EDWARD PORTIUS LANGLEY

CONTENTS

THE MAN
IN LONELY LAND

THE MAN
IN LONELY LAND

GENERAL

M R. WINTHROP LAINE threw his gloves on the table, his overcoat on a chair, put his hat on the desk, and then looked down at his shoes.

"Soaking wet," he said, as if to them. "I swear this weather would ruin a Tapley temper! For two weeks rain and sleet and snow and steam heat to come home to. Hello, General! How are the legs to-night, old man?" Stooping, he patted softly the big, beautiful collie which was trying to welcome him, and gently he lifted the dog's head and looked in the patient eyes.

"No better? Not even a little bit? I'd take half if I could, General, more than half. It's hard luck, but it's worse not to know what to do for you." He turned his head from the beseeching eyes. "For the love of heaven don't look at me like that, General, don't make it—" His breath was drawn in sharply; then, as the dog made effort to bark, to raise his right paw in greeting as of old, he put it down carefully, rang the bell, walked over to the window, and for a moment looked out on the street below.

The gray dullness of a late November afternoon was in the air of New York, and the fast-falling snowflakes so thickened it that the people hurrying this way and that seemed twisted figures of fantastic shapes, wind-blown and bent, and with a shiver Laine came back and again stood by General's side.

At the door Moses, his man, waited. Laine turned toward him. "Get out some dry clothes and see what's the matter with the heat. A blind man coming in here would think he'd struck an ice-pond." He looked around and then at the darkey in front of him. "The Lord gave you a head for the purpose of using it, Moses, but you mistake it at times for an ornament. Zero weather and windows down from the top twelve inches! Has General been in here to-day?"

"No, sir. He been in the kitchen 'most all day. You told me this morning to put fresh air in here and I put, but me and General ain't been in here since I clean up. He's been powerful poorly to-day, sir."

"I see he has." Laine's hand went to the dog and rested a moment on his head. "Close up those windows and turn on the lights and see about the heat. This room is almost as cheerful as a morgue at daybreak."

"I reckon you done took a little cold, sir." Moses closed the windows, drew the curtains, turned on more heat, and made the room a blaze of light. "It's a very spacious room, sir, and for them what loves books it's very aspirin', but of course in winter-time a room without a woman or a blazin' fire in it ain't what it might be. Don't you think you'd better take a little something, sir, to het you up inside?"

Laine, bending over General, shook his head. "No, I don't. I want sleep. I came home early to try and get a little, but—"

"You ain't had none to speak of for 'most a week." Moses still lingered. "I wish you'd let General come in my room to-night. You

3

can't stand seein' him suffer, and you'll be sick yourself if you keep a-waitin' on him all night. Can't I get you a little Scotch, sir, or a hot whiskey punch? I got the water waitin'. They say now whiskey ain't no permanent cure for colds, but it sure do help you think it is. Experience is better than expoundin' and—"

Again Laine shook his head. "Get me some dry clothes," he said, then went to the table and looked over the letters laid in a row upon it. "Have a taxi-cab here by quarter past six and don't come in again until I ring. I'm going to lie down."

A few minutes later, on a rug-covered couch, General on the floor beside him, he was trying to sleep. He was strangely tired, and for a while his only well-defined feeling was one of impatience at having to go out. Why must people do so many things they don't want to do? He put out his hand and smoothed softly General's long ears. Why couldn't a man be let alone and allowed to live the way he preferred? Why— "Quit it," he said, half aloud. "What isn't Why in life is Wherefore, and guessing isn't your job. Go to sleep."

After a while he opened his eyes and looked around the book-lined walls. When he first began to invest in books he could only buy one at a time, and now there was no room for more. He wondered if there was anything he could buy to-day that would give him the thrill his first books had given. He had almost forgotten what a thrill could mean. But who cared for books nowadays? The men and women he knew, with few exceptions, wouldn't give a twist of their necks to see his, would as soon think of reading them as of talking Dutch at a dinner-party, and very probably they were right. Knowledge added little to human happiness. Science and skill could do nothing for General. Poor General! Again he smoothed the latter's head. For years he had barked his good-bye in the morning, for years watched eagerly his coming, paws on the window-sill as dusk grew on, for years leaped joyously to meet him on his return, but he would do these things no longer. There was no chance of betterment, and death would be a mercy—a painless death which could be arranged. But he had said no, said it angrily when the doctor so suggested, and had tried a new man, who was deceiving him.

"You are all I have, General"—his hand traveled softly up and down the length of the dog's back—"and somewhere you must wait for me. I've got to stay on and play the game, and it's to be played straight, but when it's called I sha'n't be sorry."

From a box on a table close to him he took a cigar, lighted it, and watched its spirals of smoke curl upward. Life and the smoke that vanisheth had much in common. On the whole, he had no grievance against life. If it was proving a rather wearisome affair it was doubtless his own fault, and yet this finding of himself alone at forty was hardly what he had intended. There was something actually comic about it. That for which he had striven had been secured, but for what? Success unshared is of all things ironic, and soon not even General would be here to greet him when the day's work was done. He blew out a thin thread of smoke and followed its curvings with half-shut eyes. He had made money, made it honestly, and it had brought him that which it brought others, but if this were all life had to give— He threw his cigar away, and as General's soft breathing reached him he clasped his hands at the back of his head and stared up at the ceiling.

Why didn't he love his work as he used to?

6

GENERAL

He had played fair, but to play fair was to play
against the odds, and there were times when he
hated the thing which made men fight as
fiercely to-day as in the days of the jungle,
though they no longer sprang at each other's
throats. On the whole, he preferred the cave-
men's method of attack. They at least fought
face to face. As for women—

He got up, stooped down, and patted General
softly. "I'm sorry to leave you, old man, but
you'll sleep and I won't be long. Why Hope
didn't telephone what she wanted me to do,
instead of beseeching me to come to her that
she might tell me, is beyond male understanding.
But we don't try to understand women, do we,
General?"

The big brown eyes of the collie looked up in
his master's face and in them was beseeching
adoration. With painful effort he laid first one
paw and then the other on Laine's hand, and as
the latter stroked them he barked feebly.

For a moment there was silence, the silence
of understanding comrades, then Laine turned
away and began to dress.

II

ANDS in his pockets and back to the fire, Mr. Winthrop Laine looked around the room which his sister, Mrs. Channing Warrick, believed was a library, and again wondered why she had sent for him instead of telephoning what she wanted. He wasn't going to do it. That is, if it were one of the old pleadings that he would come to her parties or go to some one else's he would decline to do it, and usually the important matter on which she must see him proved something of that sort. Five years ago he had cut out things of this kind and—

"Oh, Winthrop, I'm so glad you've come!"

Laine stooped and kissed his sister. "And going out to prove it." In a gown of clinging silver over soft satin she was very lovely, and as he held her off he looked at her critically. "That is a pretty dress you have on, but there

8

isn't enough of it. What on earth did you make me come for if you're going out? When a man is my age he is privileged to stay at home and enjoy himself, not—"

Mrs. Channing Warrick stopped the buttoning of her long white gloves and looked up in her brother's face. "Do you enjoy yourself when you stay at home?"

"I enjoy myself much more at home than in other people's houses. Where are you going to-night?"

"To the Warings. There'll be cards after dinner. I suppose you declined."

"I wasn't invited."

"Hilda wanted you, but knew it was useless." Again the big blue eyes were raised to her brother's. "What makes you so horrid, Winthrop? If you go on ignoring people as you do—"

"I'll have to have paid pall-bearers at my funeral, won't I? Not a bad idea. Well, why this summons to-night?"

Mrs. Warrick pressed the last button of her glove securely, eased her skirt over her hips, and sat down carefully. "To ask you to do something for me," she said. "Channing won't be back until to-morrow, and there is no one to meet her except Decker if you don't. Outside of an automobile Decker has no sense and—"

"Meet whom?" Laine flicked the ashes from his cigar into the grate. "Who is it you want me to meet?"

"Claudia Keith. She is a cousin of Channing's and lives somewhere in Virginia on the Rappahannock River, miles from a railroad, and has never been to New York alone before. I thought I had told you she was coming, but I see you so seldom lately that I forget what I tell you and what I don't. The children think it's inhuman. After a while you won't know how to behave in company, and what will your old books and your money matter if—"

"By and by nothing will matter, my dear, but Decker's honk will be heard before I understand what you're getting at, if you don't hurry. What do you want me to do?"

"I want you to meet the nine-fifteen train from the South and—"

"Pick out an unknown person and bring her to a hostless house? I wish I was as nice as you think I am, dear madam, but I'm not. I suppose you also want me to apologize to your guest for your absence from home, tell her a pretty fairy tale and say—"

THE REQUEST

"If you'd say the right thing I'd like you to
make up something, but you wouldn't. I certainly have no idea of breaking an engagement,
however, just to be home when a country cousin
of Channing's arrives. Being such an out-of-
the-world sort of person she may think it is
strange, so please tell her—"

"I'll tell her nothing." Laine lighted a fresh
cigar. "I'm going home."

"But you can't! You're to stay to dinner,
that's why I didn't telephone you about
Claudia. The children chose taking dinner
with you as their compensation for having
to stay in on account of the weather, and
they're hanging over the banisters this very
minute." Mrs. Warrick got up and with
care straightened her skimpy skirts. "Please
don't let them eat too much. They can
have—"

"Not a bit more than they want." Laine
took the white fur coat which the maid had
laid on the chair a minute before and held it
for his sister to put on. "All this sloppy stuff
given to children of the present day will mean
anemic men and women to-morrow. I'll take
dinner with them, and if they are sick I'll take
the blame, but not if the Virginian has opinions

11

of her own concerning modern manners. Are
you sure you're well wrapped?"

"Sure. I hope Decker can find her, but I
doubt it. Maybe she can manage by herself.
Anyway, I've done all I could. Good night, and
please don't let the children eat too much of a
mixture. You'll come and see Claudia, won't
you?"

Laine shook his head. "I haven't time."

"Time! Of all nonsense!" She turned and
kissed him. "The children will have you at
dinner, anyhow, and that's why I sent for you.
Good night, mean man!"

She gathered up her skirts, and Laine, following her to the door, at which the second man
stood waiting to throw a roll of carpet down
the snow-sprinkled steps to the car at the curb,
watched it until the corner was turned, then
walked toward the dining-room, where two
young people threw two pair of arms around his
legs and rent the air with two ecstatic shrieks.

"There's turkey and giblet gravy and salad
and loads of things, Uncle Winthrop, and I am
going to sit at the head of the table, and
Timkins says I may pour the coffee for you in
the library, and—"

"Mother said I could have some ice-cream

12

and two pieces of cake if they weren't very big."
And Channing Warrick, Junior, aged seven,
made effort to remove Dorothea Warrick, aged
ten, from her point of vantage next her uncle's
right hand. But breath was lost in the high
toss given him by the strong arms which had
sent him in the air, and as he landed on his feet
he laughed in gasping delight.

"Come on." Dorothea's voice was eager.
"It's ready, and so am I, and at eight we've
got to be in bed."

III

A S he took his seat at the perfectly appointed table, Mr. Winthrop Laine nodded at first one child and then the other. "What very piggy relations I have," he said, opening his napkin. "Not a word of greeting to an ancient uncle, but just an announcement of what there is to eat. One would think you were starving."

"We are." Dorothea laid down her napkin and got up. "Excuse me for leaving my seat, but mother said we could have a good time to-night, and we can't if we're particular about manners. I hate manners. I guess I get it from you, Uncle Winthrop. I heard Miss Robin French say you didn't have any. She said she'd invited you to her house a dozen times, and you'd never been once, or made a party call or anything."

"What's a party call?" Channing's mouth

14

was full of soup. "What's a party call, Uncle
Winthrop?"

"It's the penalty one has to pay for being
invited where one doesn't want to go. What
were you saying, Dorothea?"

"I've forgotten. Channing is just as rude as
if he were somebody! Oh yes—I started to
say I'm sorry we were piggy about mentioning
the food first. We've been crazy to see you.
We had something to tell you. I think I'll sit
down here right by you; it's too far off behind
those flowers, and I'll kiss you now if you don't
mind." And Dorothea's arms were around her
uncle's neck and her cheek was laid lovingly
to his.

"Of course." Laine unfastened the arms,
drew the child's head down, kissed her, and
patted the little hands before sending their
owner to her seat. "Being the beginning of a
woman you kiss and make up, which is more
than your heathen brother does. Not another
one!" The dish of almonds was withdrawn
from Channing's reach. "Let me see your
hands, sir! And you a member of polite
society! Ah, here's the turkey. And it's the
drumstick you said you wanted, did you,
Channing? Drumsticks were put on turkeys

just for little boys. I always got the drum-stick and the gizzard."

"I don't want any drumsticks!" Channing's lips quivered. "I want—"

"And he can't have the gizzard, Uncle Winthrop, really he can't. Maybe you don't know about Fletcherizing, and you ought to be thankful you don't, but you can't Fletcherize a gizzard, not if you chew all night, and if there's breast enough for everybody, I think he'd better have that. And I'll take plenty of gravy, please, and stuffing, if there's oysters in it. Wait a minute!" Dorothea's hand went up and her head went down. I'd like to say grace: 'I thank Thee, Lord, for this sure-enough food and for Uncle Winthrop being here, and please let it happen again and don't let it make us sick. Amen.'"

Through the grace Channing's fork had been suspended, but his jaws had not stopped work; and at the last word he leaned forward and made a dive for the olives, two of which he put in his mouth at once.

To the man at the foot of the table the situation was perplexing. His niece and nephew, born of wealth and surrounded by abundance, were eating with the eagerness of little pigs;

eating as if afraid their plates would be withdrawn before they had had their fill. On the tip of Channing's nose a drop of gravy glistened in the candle-light, and Dorothea was swallowing much too rapidly for health.

Looking up, she caught her uncle's eye and leaned back in her chair. Hands on her breast and eyes half closed, she sighed regretfully. "I'm full already, and we're not half through," she said, and beckoned to the butler, who came closer. "What kind of salad is it, Timkins, and is there mayonnaise on it or that thin stuff?"

Timkins coughed slightly behind his hand. "It's mushrooms and white grapes with mayonnaise, I think, Miss, but—"

Dorothea's eyes closed tightly. "Just my luck. I've never tasted it but once, and it's perfectly grand, Uncle Winthrop. Mother had it for lunch the day that scraggy-looking woman and her daughter were here from London. Mother said she was Lady somebody, but our cook is much nicer-looking on Sundays. She didn't eat her salad."

"You ate it." Channing's fork was pointed accusingly at Dorothea. "You licked the plate."

"I certainly did." Dorothea stood up, shook

herself, sat down again, and carefully arranged her knife and fork. "We were in the pantry. Antoinette was ill and Timkins let us come in. You see, Uncle Winthrop, it's this way. We are scientifics, Channing and I. We've been brought up on a book, and we don't get enough to eat. Mother says everything has been learned out of science now—I mean about how much children can eat, and how much they can drink, and how much air they can sleep in, and how to breathe right, and Antoinette says when we were little we used to be weighed every day. And that's why we stuff so when we get a chance. I'm ten, going on eleven."

"And I'm seven, going on eight"—Channing had not yet yielded the turkey in sight for the salad to come, and his fork was still being steadily applied—"and all we have for supper—"

"Is bread and milk." Dorothea's hand waved silence to Channing. "Antoinette says the milk is magnificent, but I'd rather have something with more taste that isn't so grand. I wish I'd been born before all this science had been found out. If we sneeze we have to be sprayed, and if we cough we're sterilized or something, and the only word in the English

language Antoinette pronounces right is germs!
You'd think they were ghosts, the way she lifts
her eyes and raises her hands when she says it.
And she don't know what they are, either.
Did you kiss me when I was a baby, Uncle
Winthrop?"

"I did."

"In the mouth?"

"In the mouth."

"Well, they don't let anybody kiss babies that
way now. But if ever I have any I'm going to
let people kiss them and squeeze them, too.
I mean nice people. I don't believe in scientifics for children."

"But, my dear Miss Warrick"—Mr. Laine
was also waiting on his young nephew—"suppose your husband does. Surely a man should
have some say in the upbringing of his family!"

"Father don't." Dorothea leaned forward
and selected an olive critically. "Father would
let us have anything we want, but he says
mother must decide. He's so busy he hasn't
time to see about children. He has to make
the money to buy us—"

"Milk." Channing pushed his plate back.
"I hate milk. Gee! I'm full. You can have
my salad, Dorothea, if you'll give me your ice-

cream. It didn't make you sick the day you ate all that lady left."

"You ate leavings!" Laine's voice made effort to be horrified. "Dorothea Warrick ate leavings from a lady's plate!"

"It wasn't leavings. She didn't touch it. I was peeping through the door and I heard her say she never ate trash. It was grand. Nobody told me not to eat it, and I ate."

"An inherited habit, my dear." Laine put the almonds, the olives, and the mints beyond the reach of little arms. "Once upon a time there was a lady who lived in a garden and she ate something she ought not to have eaten and thereby made great trouble. She had been told not to, but being a woman—"

"I know about her. She was Eve." Dorothea took some almonds from her uncle's plate and put one in her mouth. "She was made out of Adam's rib, and Adam was made out of the dust of the earth. Ever since she ate that apple everybody has been made of dust, Antoinette says."

Channing sat upright, in his big blue eyes doubt and distress. "Was Dorothea and me made out of dust, Uncle Winthrop?"

"Dust, mere dust, my man."

SCIENTIFICS

For a moment there was silence and seeming thought, then Dorothea's head bobbed up and down. "Well, we can't help it, and there's no use letting things hurt that you can't help! But I don't think mother knows, Uncle Winthrop, and please don't tell her. She just hates dirt. Gracious goodness! I'm as full as a frog, and the ice-cream's got chocolate on it, too!"

In the library some minutes later Dorothea was pouring her uncle's coffee, and as he took the cup she brought him he bowed ceremoniously, then put it down to light a cigar. There were times when he wished Dorothea were his. If she were his— He took a long whiff of his cigar and threw the match in the fire.

IV

DOROTHEA AND MR. LAINE

"P ARDONNEZ-MOI!" Mademoiselle Antoinette stood at the door. Around and about her hung blushing apology, and her hands clasped and unclasped in nervous appeal. The hour had struck and her little charges must come. Would Monsieur pardon? She was so sorry, it was sad, but Madame would not like it.

"Oh, of course!" Laine waved his hand. "Good night, Buster!" Channing was tossed in the air. "If the gobblers get you to-night, don't mind. They're just turkey. Good night, Miss Wisdom!" Stooping, he kissed Dorothea and unwound the arms with which she clung to him. I'm sorry, child, but a bargain is a bargain, and your mother won't trust us if we don't play fair— It's after eight and—"

"But I haven't told you what was the specialest thing I had to—". Dorothea turned to the woman standing in the door holding her brother's hand; spoke to her rapidly.

"Je vous en prie, Mademoiselle Antoinette, Prenez Channing et ne m'attendez pas. Je vous rejoindrai dans un instant. J'ai quelque chose de très important à dier à mon oncle— deux minutes et j'arrive!"

Antoinette hesitated, then, with a gesture of despair, left the room; and instantly Dorothea was on a stool at her uncle's feet.

"Did you know?" Elbows on his knees and chin in the palms of her hands she looked up eagerly in his face. "Did you know my cousin Claudia was coming to-night?"

"I did."

"Isn't it grand!" Dorothea's hands came together, and in another minute she was dancing round and round the room, the tip ends of her skirt held by her fingers. "I'm crazy about my cousin Claudia. She's my only correspondent, the only one I love to write to, I mean. She writes things I like to hear about, and Christmas she sends me something I want. That's the way we began to write. She sent me a present, and father made me thank her in writing myself, and then she wrote me and we've been friends ever since."

Laine knocked the ashes from his cigar toward the grate. "I didn't know you knew Miss Keith."

"I don't. But I'm going to like her all right. Some things you know right here"— she put her hand on her breast. "Father's been wanting mother to ask her for a long time, but mother said she knew she didn't have clothes like New York people wore, and it might make her feel badly. I heard them talking one night, and father said the Keiths didn't have to depend on their clothes to show where they belonged, so mother invited her; but I don't think she wanted to very much. Do you suppose?"—she came toward him, and, with her hands on the arms of his chair, searched his face—"Do you suppose she will be very country-looking?"

"I really couldn't guess. People who live in the backwoods and miles from a railroad are not apt to be leaders of fashion. Doubtless her hands will be red and her face will be red and her hair will be red, but—"

"I don't care how red she is, I'm going to love her. I can tell by her letters!" Dorothea's shoulders were back and her eyes were shining. "And I don't see why you say things like that! I don't think you are very polite!"

"I don't, either. I think I'm very impolite. It may be, you know, that her eyes will be blue and her lips will be blue and her skin will be blue—"

"And that will be worse than red. I thought you were going to be glad she was coming. Aren't you glad?"

"Shall I tell the truth, or be polite?"

"Both."

"Impossible! If I told you I was glad I would be untruthful; if sorry, I would be impolite."

"But why aren't you glad? Are you too old to be glad over young ladies?"

Laine laughed. "I think I am. Yes, I'm sure that's what's the matter. Not for some years have I been glad over them. I don't care for girls older than you are, Dorothea. When they reach the grown-up age—"

"Claudia has reached the age of twenty-six. She told me so in one of her letters. What age have you reached, Uncle Winthrop?"

"Middle age."

"Is that very old?" Dorothea came closer, and her fingers slipped in and out of Laine's hair. "You're gray just a teensy bit, but I don't think she's a person who will mind if a

man isn't truly young. You've got such nice
strong arms, and I'm not afraid of lions or
tigers or bears or—or mice or anything when
you are with me. Please like her, Uncle Winthrop!" Dorothea's face was pressed against
Laine's. "Next to father and mother and
Channing I love you best, and I think I'm
going to love her next after you."

"Mademoiselle Dorothea!"

From the steps outside Antoinette was calling, and Dorothea nodded her head at her
uncle. "That's another thing my children are
not going to have. They are never going to
have a French governess to put them to bed
and make them say their prayers in French.
I don't believe the Lord likes it. Good night,
Uncle Winthrop. I hope my cousin Claudia
will be politer about you than you've been
about her, and I know she hasn't red hands."
She waved her own and threw a kiss, but as
she reached the door Laine called her back.

"Come here, Dorothea."

She turned and came toward him. "Did
you call me, Uncle Winthrop?"

"I did." He drew her on his knees. "Did
you say you said your prayers in French?"

"Every night, unless for punishment I have

to say a German one. Channing just shuffles his out and runs all the words together so I don't believe even God can understand them. I don't like French prayers."

"Then why do you say them?"

"Oh, we have to! All the children I know say their prayers in French. One day six of us had a race to see which could say them fastest and say the most. I beat. Want to hear me?"

"Indeed I don't!" Laine's voice was emphatic. "But I don't like French prayers for little American girls. I never cared for parrots or—"

"What kind do you say, French or American?" Dorothea was stroking her uncle's fingers one by one. "I always say my real prayers inside after I get in bed—that is, if I'm not too sleepy; and they're just plain talking to the Lord. You see, we are not allowed to speak one word except in French to Antoinette, and mother likes us to speak it to her, only she is always in such a hurry she forgets half the time. We speak English to father, all right, though; father says French for breakfast is all foolishness, and I think so, too. We take breakfast with father every morning, and we

just have a grand time. Mother is never very
well in the mornings, so she don't get up; but
we take lunch with her when there isn't company and she isn't going out. Did you know
the Dufferns had a new baby at their house?".

Laine shook his head.

"They have. It's a girl. They had four
girls already, and Julia says they're going to
change their doctor. He always brings girls.".

"Madam-oiselle Dor-othea!"

Dorothea slipped from her uncle's lap. "I
know what that means. Whenever she says
'Madam-ois-elle Doro-thea!' through her nose
it's a German prayer. Good night.". And this
time she was gone.

Laine followed her to the steps to take upon
himself the responsibility of her delay, and as
he came back in the room he glanced at the
clock and took out his watch. It wouldn't do
for a girl from the country to get into New
York alone at this time of night, and, of course,
he would have to meet her; but why did she
come at this hour of night? Ringing for his
coat and hat, he put them on, then stopped to
light a cigar, and as the match was held to it
the front door-bell rang sharply. A moment
later some one was talking to Timkins.

DOROTHEA AND MR. LAINE

"Is this Mr. Warrick's residence?"

The voice that asked the question was fresh and clear, and carried easily to where he stood. He looked around quickly as if for escape.

"Yes'm." He could picture the bow Timkins was making. Timkins was the politest person he knew. "Yes'm, and this is Miss Keith, isn't it? Just come in, ma'm, we're expecting of you, though your train must have been a little earlier than usual, ma'm. Mr. Warrick is out of town, and Mrs. Warrick had a pressing engagement which couldn't be denied, but she left messages for you, and I think a note. Yes'm, just this way." And Timkins, knowing Laine was in the library, led the stranger past the door and up the steps, over the banisters of which was heard from Dorothea a cry of delight.

"Oh, my Cousin Claudia! My Cousin Claudia! I'm so glad you've come! I'm so glad!"

A laugh as fresh as the dawn of perfect morning followed the kisses next heard, and then the new voice spoke again.

"You precious child! I'm so glad you're glad. It's so nice to have somebody glad to see you!"

V

THE LOSS OF HIS BEST FRIEND

AT the click of Laine's latch-key Moses started from the doze into which he had fallen and jumped to his feet. "Lord, sir, I sure is glad you've come," he said, following Laine into the library. "Gineral's been mighty bad off since you went away, and one time I thought he was plumb gone. He done had what you might call a faintin' fit if'n he was a person."

"Where is he?" Laine's voice was quick, and his eyes swept the room. "What have you done for him?"

"He laid himself on the rug in your room, sir, and I give him a little brandy and water. Most in general that will hit the spot and—"

But Laine was in his room, and Moses, following, saw him on his knees by the rug, his right arm under the dog's head, his left on

30

the heart which was barely beating, and softly he tiptoed out again.

For an hour or so he stayed away, wandering between his room and the kitchen, the kitchen and the dining-room, and back again to his room, talking to himself in an undertone; and presently he sat down by a table and began to turn the pages of a family Bible which adorned it, and which he had presented to himself the Christmas before.

"It do beat all how he love that dog," he said, as if to some one at his side, "and it's a-goin' to make a hole in his heart when he's gone. I never seen anybody set such store on a thing what ain't a human being as he do on Gineral, and as for Gineral—if a dog could do what you call worship, he sure do worship Mr. Laine. They was partners, them two, and it will be a quiet place when Gineral ain't here any more."

Slowly he turned page after page of the big-printed Bible, with its illuminated text; but presently he closed it. "I've read right much of it, and I've heard a heap of it expounded, but I haven't got no recollections of any references to the passing of dogs in it," he continued, taking out a plug of tobacco and cutting off a good-sized piece. "I wish there was. When something you love is leavin' you, you have a mighty sinkin' feeling in the pit of your stomach, and a terrible understandin' of the unableness of man. And then it is you feel a reachin' out after something what ain't man. Mr. Laine is mighty learned, but learn-in' ain't no cure for loneliness, and Gineral is all he's got. And I tell you now, this comin' home to empty rooms is cold comin'.".

Moses was speaking to the wall opposite, but the wall not replying he got up and tip-toed to Laine's bedroom. Looking up, Laine saw him and called him in.

"Go to bed, Moses," he said, and his voice was very tired. "There is nothing you can do. If I need you I will let you know."

Moses shook his head. "I ain't a-goin' to bed, Mr. Laine. You can make me go out if you want to, but if I ain't intrudin' I would like to stay.".

Slowly the hours passed. From the street occasional stirrings reached them faintly; but in the room only short breathing broke the silence. As day dawned Moses, from his seat near the door, spoke:

"Mr. Laine?".

"Well." Laine did not look up.

"When dogs die do they live again?"

"I don't know."

"I don't reckon anybody knows. But that don't mean they don't. If I was as certain I was fixed for heaven as I know Gineral is a-goin' to be waitin' for you somewhere, I'd feel more reconcilement to death. Some things can die and some things can't. There ain't no time limit to love, Mr. Laine. I think"— Moses got up—"I think Gineral is trying to make you understand something, sir."

Half an hour later Laine called Moses back into the room, gave a few orders, changed his clothes, and without waiting for breakfast went out, and not until dark did he come in again.

Dinner was a pretense, and presently he pushed his coffee aside, lighted a cigar, and took up the evening paper. The headlines were glaring, but he passed them quickly. Telegraphic news was skimmed, stock reports and weather conditions glimpsed unheedingly, and the editorial page ignored, and, finally, with a gesture of weariness, he threw the paper on the floor and went into the library.

It was, as Moses had said, a very spacious

room, and its furnishings were distinctive; but, though warm and brightly lighted, to stay in it to-night was impossible, and, ringing for his coat and hat, he made ready to go out.

At the table he lingered a moment and glanced at some letters upon it. Mechanically he took one up, looked at the writing of his name, and wondered indifferently who it was from. Breaking it open, he read the few words it contained, and at them his face colored and he bit his lips to hide their twitching. He read:

DEAR MR. LAINE,—Dorothea has just told me. I am so sorry. CLAUDIA KEITH.

With a sudden surrender to something stubbornly withheld, he sat down in the chair near the table, leaned back in it, and closed his eyes to keep back that which stung and blinded them. To most of his friends the going of General would be but the going of a dog, and barely a passing thought would be its portion when they heard, but she must understand. He got up. No. There was no one who could really understand.

VI

A LETTER FROM DOROTHEA

FOR a moment he hesitated whether to go down or up the street. The air was biting, but the snow, fairly well cleaned from the sidewalks, no longer bothered; and, crossing into Madison Avenue, he turned down and began to walk rapidly toward that part of the city where there would be few people and little glare, and as he walked unconsciously he repeated over and over to himself: "Dorothea has just told me. I am so sorry."

"Mister, please, sir, buy a paper?" He stopped abruptly. The boy in front of him stamped first one foot and then the other, and the hand he held out was rough and red. Drawing it back he blew on it for a little warmth.

"What are you doing out this time of night?"

Laine asked the question hardly knowing why.
"You ought to be home in bed."

"Ain't got no home." The boy laughed
cheerfully, and again put his fist to his mouth
and blew upon it. "I'm sleepin' with another
boy this week, but I have to pay him. Please
buy a paper, Mister!"

Under his breath Laine caught himself saying something, then handed the boy a piece of
money and passed on. Where was he, anyhow?
Surely he was in no mood for the life of this
neighborhood. It was one he had seldom
been in, and as he looked at its houses dull
wonder filled him as to their occupants. To
keep breath in their bodies meant sordid
struggle and bitter strife, but possibly they
were happy. Certainly he had long since
learned the possession of mere material things
did not mean happiness. He had long since
learned a great many things it was unfortunate
to know.

A clock in the church near by struck ten,
and turning he went over into the Avenue and
began his walk up-town. As he reached Madison Square he looked at the empty benches and
wondered as to the fate of the derelicts who
daily filled them in warm weather, and won-

dered if they, too, wondered what it was all for—this thing called life.

In contrast to the traffic of the day the stillness of the Avenue was puzzling. Only the whir of an automobile or the occasional hoofbeats of a cab-horse broke the silence, and hardly less dark than the tenements just passed were its handsome houses, with their closed shutters and drawn curtains, and the restless occupants therein. As he reached the Park he stopped, hesitated, and lighted a fresh cigar. Three squares away was his sister's house, and in it was the girl with the fresh, clear voice. He took the note she had sent him out of his pocket, and in the light hanging just above him looked again at the firm, clear writing, then put it back. Did she, too, wonder at life, at its emptiness and aimlessness? Her voice did not sound as if she were tired of it or found it wearisome. It sounded like a very happy voice.

At his door he turned the latch-key, and for a moment—a bare moment—drew back; then, with a shiver, he opened the door and went inside.

Moses was waiting. "Miss Dorothea she called me up, sir, and told me to be sure and

give you this letter to-night. She slip out of
bed to telephone when that French white lady
was out the room, she say. She had her Ma
send it by messenger, and she was so 'fraid
you wouldn't get it to-night she couldn't sleep.
She sent a peck of love."

Laine took the letter and went to his room.
Dorothea was given to letters, and if his absence was unduly long a communication to
that effect was promptly received. He had
seen her last night, however. What was she
wanting now? Breaking the seal, he read the
sprawly writing with narrowed eyes, then read
again, that he might miss no word.

DEAR UNCLE WINTHROP,—Moses telefoned us and
Channing and I have just cried and cried and cried. But
I won't even call his name if you will only come and let
me kiss you so you will know. We wanted to send you
some flowers but Claudia said our love was best. She
is so sorry too. She had one and it died last spring. I
had a headake to-day. It came from my heart because
of you and she made it go away. I think she could make
most any kind of pain go away. And her hands are not
red and her hair is brown and her lashes are brown too,
and long and lovely. I don't know the color of her
eyes. I think they are glad color. I love her! I knew
I would.

Your devoted niece, DOROTHEA.

P. S.—I told her you didn't like young ladies and she
said she didn't like old gentlemen, except a few. Please,

A LETTER FROM DOROTHEA

P-L-E-A-S-E come and see me—and you can come in
the nursery if you don't want to see her. She knows.
Your loving niece,

DOROTHEA.

P. S. Again.—You ought to hear her laugh. Its
delishus.

He put the letter back in the envelope, and
the envelope in his pocket. "She knows," he
repeated. What under heaven had Dorothea
been telling her? He must see Dorothea and
have it stopped. Did she think him a feeble
and infirm person who leaned on a stick, or a
crabbed and cross one who had no manners?
He would have to call, if only to thank her
for her note. No. He would do that in
writing. Next week, perhaps, he might drop
in and see Dorothea. But Hope and Channing
should take the girl about, show her the city.
Certainly Hope could not be so idiotic as to
let clothes matter. In his sister's world clothes
were the insignia of its order, and of late Hope
had shown signs that needed nipping. He
must see Hope. Next week would be time
enough, but Hope and Dorothea must both be
seen.

VII

"HOW do you do? Oh, how do you do, too, Miss Keith?" Miss Robin French held out a hand first to Mrs. Channing Warrick and then to her guest and shook their hands with vigor. "Did you ever know such weather at this season of the year? Even heat and cold are no longer like they used to be. Everything is intensified. Indeed I will have some tea! No lemon, and one lump. *One.* That's a sick-looking fire, Hope. Good gracious! I just did catch that vase of flowers! Such a stupid fancy, putting flowers everywhere for people to knock over. Well, Miss Keith, have you gotten your breath since you reached New York? Something of a town, isn't it?"

A gulp of hot tea, taken standing by Miss French, gave pause for a moment, and Claudia Keith instinctively drew her feet up under her chair behind the tea-table. To duck her head, as one would dodge an on-coming deluge, was an impulse, but only with her feet could effort be made for self-preservation, and as she refilled the cup held out to her by the breezy visitor she blessed the table which served as a breastwork of defense. With a hasty movement she put in the one lump and handed the cup back. "I breathe here very well," she said, and smiled into the scrutinizing eyes. "New York is very wonderful."

"And very disagreeable eight months out of the twelve." Miss French put her cup on the table, threw her fur coat on the chair behind her, sat down, and, taking the cup again, drank its entire contents. "Pretty good tea, Hope; at most places it's undrinkable." Again she handed the cup to Claudia. "One more and that's all. I'm cutting out tea a bit—only twelve cups a day now."

"Twelve!" The exclamation was beyond recall. Claudia's hand stopped in its pouring. "Twelve!"

"That's what I said. Have taken thirty many times, but the doctor thought I was getting nerves and called me down. Nerves!" Miss French's nose went up. "Nerves and

4   41

nonsense are twin sisters, and I've no opinion of either. How did you like the opera last night?"

The question being addressed apparently to the cigarette Miss French took out of a little silver case, lighted, and began to smoke, neither Mrs. Warrick nor Miss Keith answered, each waiting for the other; but it did not matter, Miss French was looking at a photograph in front of her. With lorgnette to her eyes, she examined it critically.

"Rather a good picture of your brother, Hope. Didn't know he'd do anything so human as have a picture taken." She took it up. "Winthrop would hardly take prizes at a beauty show, but he's certainly all there for something better. When did you get this?"

"A month ago, I guess." Mrs. Warrick took a log from the basket on the hearth and put it on the andirons. "The editors of the *Review* made him send his picture when that article of his came out on 'Tax Terrors and Tax Traditions.' Channing says it's the best thing that's been written on taxation for years, and in banking circles—"

"He's earned his pedestal." Miss French

42

put down her cigarette and handed the case to Claudia.

"Smoke?"

Claudia shook her head. "Thanks. I don't—"

"Pity. You've lots to learn yet. Most of you Southerners have, but when you catch up you speed all right. I'll give you this for nothing—don't toboggan all at once. Have you seen this picture of Hope's crank of a brother? You needn't expect to meet him. He comes of good Vermont stock, and its granite is no firmer than his principles; but he has no manners. I've known him fifteen years and am qualified to speak."

"He has got manners!" Mrs. Warrick turned indignantly toward Miss French. "Claudia only got here Thursday night, and Winthrop has been too busy—"

"Busy! You're dippy about Winthrop, Hope. He's the most indifferent human being to other human beings that walks this earth, and has more friends—men friends—than any man I know. He's rotten spoiled; that's what's the matter with him. He's been chased, I admit. What uncaught man of means isn't? I've no patience with Winthrop. It's natural young girls should bore him, but that's no rea-

43

son why he should live so entirely to himself."

"Perhaps"—Claudia took up a letter from
the table in front of her and with it tapped her
lips absently—"perhaps he prefers to live that
way. I wonder, Miss French, if you can tell me
where Kroonstater's is? No one here seems to
to know, and every day I get further commissions
from my county which can only be filled there.
Years ago some one from Brooke Bank bought
wonderful and marvelous Christmas things from
Kroonstater's, and ever since it's been the one
store in New York for many of our people. I
must find it."

"Kroonstater's?" Miss French again put
up her lorgnette. "Never heard of it."

Claudia laughed. "I see you, too, have
something to learn. You don't know the joy
of shopping if you don't know a store of that
kind. I suppose I'll have to find it by myself."

"For goodness' sake don't, Claudia." Mrs.
Warrick got up; some one at the telephone
wanted her. "I passed one of those down-
town stores once, and the crowd in it was something awful. You never know what kind of
disease you might catch, and the people are so

pushy. All the nice stores have Christmas things."

"I don't doubt it." Claudia smiled. " But Brooke Bank people have ideas of their own. Their demands are many, and their dollars few. And, then, I love to see the crowd. Their pennies are as important as our pounds, and to watch their spending is the best kind of a play."

"Where did you say you came from?" Miss French surveyed the girl in front of her with sudden interest. Something new under the sun was ever the quest of her inquiries and pursuits, and as if she had possibly found it she looked closer at her friend's guest. Not the youth, not the fair skin now flushed with color that came and went, nor the long dark lashes, nor perfect teeth, nor anything that could be named made the girl distinctive, but something well-defined and penetrating. Again she asked the question. "Where did you say you were from?"

"From Virginia. Have you ever been there?"

Miss French shook her head.

Claudia sat up. In her eyes no longer laughter, and incredulity that was genuine. "You mean you *never* have been to Virginia?"

"Never."

Elbows on the table and chin in the palms of

her hands, Claudia looked at Miss French as
intently as Miss French looked at Claudia.
"Then you've never heard, I suppose, of the
Northern Neck, or Westmoreland County, or
Essex, or Lancaster, or King George, or—"

"Never. Quite English, aren't they? Is
that where you live?"

"I live in Essex. We're on the Rappahannock. There isn't a railroad in the county.
We have to take the boat for Fredericksburg or
Norfolk to get anywhere, unless we cross the
river into Westmoreland County and drive over
to the Potomac side and make the boat to
Washington. Have you ever been to Washington?"

"Of course. I've been pretty well over the
world."

"And left out its best part!" Claudia
laughed and got up to turn the logs which were
smoking. "You mustn't die before seeing it.
There isn't so much to see, perhaps, but a
good deal to feel. Do you like fox-hunting?"

"Never tried it." Again Miss French looked
at the girl now standing in front of her. She
was certainly not a plate of fashion—that is, not
a French plate—but she was graceful, and her
clothes were really very good. Her uncon-

sciousness of self was rather astounding in a country girl.

"I think you'd like a fox-hunt. I will miss the big one this year—Thanksgiving comes so late, and Christmas there's no time."

"Christmas in the country must be very stupid."

"Stupid!" Claudia's hands, which had been clasped behind her back, opened and came together on her breast. "Of course"—her eyes were raised to Miss French's—"it's a point of view, I suppose. We don't think it's stupid. We love it."

Miss French got up, put her cigarette-case in her velvet hand-bag, slipped on her coat, fastened her veil, picked up her muff, shook it, and looked toward the door, between whose curtains Mrs. Warrick was standing.

"I thought you'd gone for good, Hope. You must have been telling all you knew, and more. Miss Keith was just saying she loved Christmas in the country. I can't imagine anything worse, unless it's Christmas in town. I hate Christmas! If I could go to sleep a week before, and not wake up until a week after, I'd surely do it. Why, Winthrop Laine!"

On her way to the door Miss Robin French

stood still and looked at the man coming in; and over her ruddy face swept color, almost purple in its deepness. She was a handsome woman, stubbornly resisting the work of time. In her eyes was restless seeking, in her movements an energy that could not be exercised in the limits of her little world; and Claudia, watching her, felt sudden whimsical sympathy. She was so big, so lordly, so hungrily unhappy.

She held out her hand. "How do you do?" she said. "I am just going home, as your sister hasn't asked me to dinner. I suppose you will stay—"

"If there's to be any dinner. Hope has a way of cutting it out every now and then." He turned to his sister. "Are you going out to-night?"

"I certainly am not, and I'm so glad you've come! I've lots to tell you and ask you. Won't you stay, Robin?" The question was put feebly. "Do stay. Oh, I beg your pardon, Claudia, you were so far off! You haven't met my brother. Winthrop, this is Channing's cousin, Miss Keith. Please give him some tea, Claudia. I know he's frozen. Can't you stay, Robin—really?"

"Really nothing! Good-bye." Miss French

48

waved her muff to the man who, over the tea-cups, was shaking hands with the girl on the opposite side of the table, and shook her head as he started toward her. "Don't come, Jenkins is out there with the car. I'd stay to dinner, but Hope doesn't enjoy hers if there's a high-neck dress at the table. Good-bye, Miss Keith; see you to-morrow night, I suppose." And, like a good strong draught that passes, she was gone.

"I'm glad she had sense enough not to stay." Mrs. Warrick came toward the tea-table. "I'm fond of Robin, but of late she's been even more energetic and emphatic than usual, and I feel like I'm being battledored and shuttlecocked whenever I see her. Why don't you drink your tea, Winthrop?"

"I don't believe I put any sugar in it. I beg your pardon!" Claudia took up the sugar-bowl. "It was Miss French, I guess. She's such a—such a gusty person. I love to hear her talk. How many, Mr. Laine?"

"Three, please, and no comments, Hope. If a man must drink tea he ought to have all the sugar he wants. That last lump was so very little I think you might put in another, Miss Keith. Thank you. Perhaps this is sweet enough."

49

"Winthrop just takes tea to have the sugar. He's as bad as Dorothea about sweet things." Mrs. Warrick turned to her brother. "Are you really going to stay to dinner? Please do. This is the only evening we're to be home for a week, and Channing is anxious to see you on some business."

"Is he?" Laine put down his cup. "Well, he won't see me on business to-night. I've an office down-town. In your part of the world, Miss Keith, don't you ever let men have a chance to forget there's such a thing as business?"

Claudia got up. "I'm afraid they have too much chance." She put her hand lightly on Mrs. Warrick's arm. "Will you excuse me, Hope? I have a letter to write." She bowed slightly in Laine's direction and was gone before he could reach the door to draw aside the curtains for her.

Mrs. Warrick leaned back in her chair and crossed her arms. "Do sit down, Winthrop, and let's talk. I'm so glad to have a little time alone with you. I so seldom have it that—"

"Your guest was certainly not slow in giving it to you. She could hardly do anything but leave after your insistence upon having things to tell me. What in the name of Heaven did you do that for? Does she think we don't know how to behave up here?"

"Oh, she understands! She knows you didn't come to see her, and, besides, she's gone up-stairs to write to her mother. If King George had been here she'd have gone. You know, I really dreaded her coming, but I needn't. She has been to a good many places— was abroad for a year with one of her sisters whose husband was secretary or something to one of our ministers or somebody—but she doesn't know New York at all. She's met a number of her friend's friends already, and I won't have to scoop up men for her. Last night at the Van Doren's she had more around her than she could talk to. Always has had, Channing says. She'll be no bother; and don't stay away because she's here. Tell me"— she put her hand on his knee—"is it true you are going to Panama next month? Robin French told me she heard you would leave on the twelfth."

"If Miss French could sell fairy tales as rapidly as she can repeat them she'd make a fortune. I have no idea what I am going to do next month."

"I wish I didn't know I was going to Savannah for Christmas. It's Channing's year, and of course we ought to go to his mother, as she is too old to come to us, but there's so much going on, and then you'll be alone."

"Oh, I'll manage all right. The one good thing about Christmas is it doesn't last long." He leaned forward and with the tongs turned a smoldering log. "But it's incomprehensible how a woman with a home can keep up this everlasting going to other people's houses. To-morrow night you go—"

"To the Taillors. Mrs. Taillor's débutante daughter makes her first bow to—"

"Capitalized society, does she? Poor child! The pains of pleasure are many."

"They surely are! She looks like a scared rabbit, and I heard her say only a week ago she'd rather die than be a débutante. But she'll get on. Her mother will corral the men and compel them to come in and pay her attention. Are you going?"

"Hardly." Laine looked at his watch. "What time do you have dinner?"

"Seven. It's time for me to dress." Mrs. Warrick got up. "Do pray be decent and go to-morrow night, Winthrop. Mr. Taillor has

been such a good friend, and Mrs. Taillor will
be so pleased. Don't forget to send the child
flowers. I wonder if Claudia is ready. Dorothea grabs her every chance she gets, and I
don't doubt she's with the children this minute.
She'll stay until dinner is served, so don't
worry; and for goodness' sake don't let her
being here keep you away."

VIII

THE RECEPTION

OMING down the crowded steps into the crowded drawing-room, Winthrop Laine slowly made his way through the door to the place where Mr. and Mrs. Taillor and their daughter were receiving their guests and passing them on with a rapidity that would have been creditable to the custodian of a game of human roulette, and as he reached them his name was called with uncomfortable clearness.

"Well, this *is* a surprise!" Both of Mrs. Taillor's hands held Laine's. "But commend me to a person who knows when to change his mind. Jessica, you should feel honored. Awfully good of you to come! How do you do, Mrs. Haislip?" And Laine, too, was passed on, and a moment later found himself in a corner where he could watch the door and all who came in.

THE RECEPTION

What was he here for? He didn't know. The air was heavy with perfume. In the distance music reached him faintly, and the throb and stir and color and glow for some minutes interested him as he glanced around the handsome room with its massed palms, its wealth of flowers, its brilliant lights, and streams of gorgeously gowned women and prosperous-looking men, and then he wondered what had made him start anything of this sort again. To come had been a sudden decision. Long ago the dreariness of functions such as these had caused their giving-up, but a fancy to look once more upon one had possessed him unaccountably, and he had come.

Up-stairs in the men's room his reappearance had been banteringly commented on, and with good-natured hand-shaking he had been welcomed back; but down here many faces were strange and figures unrecognizable; and with something of shock he realized how few were the years necessary to change the personnel of any division of humanity. The heat was intense, and moving farther back toward a screen of palms near a half-open window, he pulled one slightly forward that he might see and not be seen, and again watched each new-

comer with mild speculation as to whether he
or she were known or not.

For a while it was puzzling, this continuing
arrival of new faces, with here and there one he
knew well or slightly; but gradually its effect
chilled, and he was wondering if he could get
away when he heard his name called.

"Winthrop Laine! Of all people!" Miss
French held out her hand. "From what loop-
hole were you watching this passing show for
man's derision given? May I come in?"

"You may."

Miss French moved behind the palms and
pushed a tall leaf aside. "You and I are too
old for these things, Winthrop. I don't know
why I come—to get away from myself, I suppose. Look at that Miss Cantrell! She pa-
rades her bones as if they were a private collection of which she was proud! And did you
ever see anything as hideous as that gown Miss
Gavins has on? Paris green couldn't be more
deadly. I heard Mathilda Hickman tell her
just now to be sure and wear it to her dinner
next week, it was so becoming; and only yesterday she was shrieking over it at a luncheon
where everybody was talking about it. Mr.
Trehan is to be at the dinner, and Mathilda

56

wants every woman to look her worst. Hello! There comes Channing and Hope and the cousin from the country. Rather a nice sort of person, awfully young and inexperienced, but—" She put up her lorgnette. "They are talking to Miss Cantrell. Miss Keith is not becoming to Miss Cantrell, or Miss Gavins, either. Her shoulders are excellent and her head perfectly poised. That white dress suits her. Have you been in the dining-room?"

Laine came from behind the palms. "No; I was to wait for Hope. Awfully glad to have seen you, Robin. A stranger in a strange land has a chance, but a man who has lost his place hasn't. People have a way of closing up if you lose step, and I"—he laughed—"I lost step long ago. I'll see you again." And, watching, Miss French saw him take possession of Miss Keith and go with her out of the room.

Half an hour later Laine found a chair for Claudia at the end of the hall opposite the dining-room, and as she sat down he wiped his forehead. "I used to play football, but—"

"You're out of practice? I don't believe you did take more than three men by the shoulders and put them aside. I don't understand football very well, but a dining-room seems to be the center-rush. Please look at that crowd over there!" She nodded toward the open door, through which a mass of men could be seen struggling. "Isn't it queer—the eagerness with which a plate of salad is pursued?"

"And the earnestness with which it is devoured." Laine put his handkerchief in his pocket. Will you wait here a moment until I can get you something? I'll be back—"

"Indeed I won't." Claudia stood up. "It's fun to watch, but only fruit from the tree of life would be worth a scrimmage of that kind. If I could get on top of a picture-frame or a curtain-pole, or anything from which I could look down on a show like this, I'd have a beautiful time, but"—she opened her fan—"it's rather stuffy to be in it."

Laine glanced around. He knew the house well. Next to the library, but not opening into it, was a small room of Taillor's which could only be reached by a narrow passage at their right. He walked away and looked in at the door. The room was empty.

"I think it will be more comfortable over there," he said, coming back, then saw she was talking to a man he had long known and long disliked. He stopped a servant who was passing, a man who had once been in the employ of one of his clubs. "Bring some stuff over here and be quick, will you, David?" he said, then spoke to the man talking to Miss Keith.

His greeting to Dudley was not cordial. It was with difficulty indeed that he did not take Claudia away at once. Dudley was not the sort of man for her to have anything to do with. In a time incredibly short, but to Laine irritatingly long, David was back, abundantly supplied; and with a nod he was directed to the room at the end of the narrow hall, and Laine turned to the girl at his side. "Are you ready?"

"Good night." Miss Keith held out her hand. "Bettina sent you many messages."

"I'm coming to get them—may I?" Mr. Dudley's eyes were frankly eager. "But where are you going? Laine always was a monopolist. What are you doing at a thing of this kind, anyhow, Laine? Don't pay any attention to him, Miss Keith. He's mere facts and figures, and the froth of life is not in him. I'm much better company."

The last words were lost in the push of new arrivals, and quickly Laine led the way to the room where David was waiting. Through the

open door the sound of music reached them
faintly over the shrill rise and fall of many
voices; and as Claudia sat down near the table
on which various plates had been placed she
put her hands to the sides of her face and,
laughing, drew them away.

"Did you ever put a cockle-shell to your ear
and notice its roar?" she asked. "That's how
a Tea sounds when there're only women at it.
When there're men it's more so. What is this?"
She held her fork suspended for a moment.
"It's awfully good, but very elusive. What
do you suppose it is?"

"A bunch of guesses wouldn't hit it. Clicot
is providing the provender, I believe; I see
his men here, and the ambition of Clicot's life
is to create a new dish. I'm glad you like it.
It's as near nothing as anything I ever ate.
Are you comfortable? Is that chair all right?"

Claudia nodded. "Why don't you sit down?
I'm sorry we can't see the people, but it's nice
to be out of the crowd." She looked around
the room. "This is a very handsome house.
I never saw more gorgeous flowers, and to-
morrow," she gave a queer little sigh, "to-
morrow it will all be over—and the flowers
faded."

THE RECEPTION

"Faded things are the penalties of wealth. It's the one compensation for follies of this sort that they are soon over."

"I don't think they are always follies. When I was young—"

He looked down at her, in his eyes a quiet gleam. "When you were what?"

"Young. Really young, I mean. I had my party when I was eighteen. I remember it just as well." She gave a happy little laugh. "But of course we change with time. My sister says I am developing a dreadful disease. It's a tendency. Did you ever have it?"

"A what?"

"A tendency—to think and wonder and ask questions, you know. She says people who have it are very trying. But how can you help a thing you're born with?" She leaned forward, pushed the plates aside, and folded her arms on the table. "I always wondered about things, but I didn't entirely wake up until I was over twenty. I don't blame people for having things like this"—she waved her hands inclusively—"that is, if they like this kind of thing." She looked up at him "We're just like children. All of us love to splurge every now and then. Don't we?"

"It looks that way. Splurge has a variety of forms." Laine leaned forward, hands clasped loosely between his knees. "But the tendency—is it catching?"

She laughed. "In the country it is. I live in the country, but it didn't develop in me until I had several winters in the city. I used to love things like this. I didn't know much about a good many other things, and it was when I found out that I began to look at people and wonder if they knew, and cared, and what they were doing with it—their life I mean, their chance, their time, their money. One winter it got so bad Lettice sent me home. Lettice lives in Washington; she's my second sister. My oldest sister is a widow, and is still in London, where her husband died two years ago. I kept looking for glad faces and real, sure-enough happiness; and so many people looked bored and bothered and tired that I couldn't understand—and Lettice made me go home. Her husband is in Congress, and she said I wanted to know too much."

"Have you yet found what you were looking for?" Laine leaned back in his chair and shaded his eyes with his hand.

"Yes." She laughed lightly and got up.

THE RECEPTION

"You can find anything, I guess, if you look for it right. And in such unexpected places you find things!" She stopped and listened. "I believe people are going home. Please take me to Hope. I can't imagine what made us stay in here so long!"

IX

DOROTHEA ASKS QUESTIONS

AT the library window Dorothea drew the curtains aside and looked up and down the street. Presently she blew softly upon the pane and with her finger made on it four large letters, then rubbed them out and went back to the mantel, before whose mirror, on tiptoe, she surveyed the bow on her hair and straightened it with care.

"I don't see why they don't come," she said, aggrievedly, smoothing down her skirt. "It's time, and I'm going to ring for tea, anyhow. Mother said I could pour it, and I'll play lady all by myself if nobody comes to play it with. I believe"—she turned her head—"I believe they're coming now."

Again she went to the window, then rang for tea. "Quick, Timkins; please hurry and bring it in before they come," she said. "They'll be

64

frozen." And as Timkins disappeared she put a fresh log on the fire, drew the table closer to it, and seated herself at it.

"I'm a chaperone lady. I'm chaperoning my Uncle Winthrop and my Cousin Claudia!" In gleeful delight she rocked backward and forward and twisted her hands together tightly. "I'm sorry mother has a headache, but I certainly am glad I can pour tea for them. I don't know why anybody wants to go horse-back-riding on a day like this, though; I'd freeze." She straightened the embroidered cloth on the table as Timkins put the tray on it, and lighted the lamp under the kettle, and, taking up the tea-caddy, she measured out a generous amount of its contents.

"I'll be careful and not get burnt up." She waved Timkins out. "They're coming right in. It's the funniest thing about Uncle Winthrop," she went on, as if to the tea-cups she was arranging. "He didn't want to come and see Cousin Claudia, and now he comes here every day. Wouldn't it be funny if he wanted her for a sweetheart — and wouldn't it be grand!" Her arms were thrown out and then hugged rapturously to her bosom; but instantly her face sobered. "He can't have her,

though, because she's somebody else's. I wonder if he knows? He ought to, for Miss Robin
says when he wants anything he never gives
up until he gets it, and he can't get her if she's
gotten. Mother says he just comes here and
takes her out and sends her flowers and things
because she asked him to be nice to her; but
I don't believe it's just for kindness. Gentlemen aren't kind to ladies if they don't like
them. I believe— Heigho, Cousin Claudia!"
She waved her hand from behind the table.
"Have you had a nice ride? Where's Uncle
Winthrop?"

"Coming."

Drawing off his gloves, Laine came in the
library, and as he reached the table he took
from Dorothea's hands the cup of tea just
poured and handed it to Claudia.

"Are you frozen?" His voice was slightly
worried. "We shouldn't have gone—I did
not know how very cold it was."

"It wasn't a bit too cold. I love it." Claudia shook her head. "I don't want any tea
until my hands can hold the cup, though.
They *are* cold." With her foot on the fender,
she held out first one hand and then the other
to the blazing fire and laughed in Dorothea's

wide-opened eyes. "What is it, Madam Hostess? Is anything the matter with me?"

"Your cheeks look like they're painted. They didn't when you went out."

"Do they?" Claudia put her hands to her face. "The wind did it." Taking off her hat, she laid it on the table, loosened the hair on her temples, and sat down on the tapestried footstool near the hearth. "I'll have some tea now, please. Are there any sandwiches? I'm starving. Where's your mother, Dorothea?"

"Sick. Got a headache. I'm to pour tea, unless you'd rather." She got up reluctantly. "Would you?"

"Indeed I wouldn't." Claudia waved her back. "You suit that table beautifully. When you're a real grown-up lady you won't leave out anything; but this time you forgot the sugar."

"Did I? I was thinking of something else, I guess." Two lumps were put in the cup Laine handed her. "Where did you all go this afternoon?"

Claudia looked at Laine. "I don't know the names of the places around here. Where did we go?"

"We went—" Laine put his cup on the table and, drawing a chair closer to the fire, sat down. "I've forgotten the name of the road."

"Forgotten!" Dorothea stopped the rattling of the spoons. "You told me once you knew all the roads within twenty miles of New York in the pitch-dark. I think it's very funny you don't know where you've been. You couldn't have been looking much."

"We didn't look at all. It was too cold—" Laine put another log on the fire—"the roads were frozen, and to keep the horses from slipping was all we could attend to."

"Couldn't you talk?"

"Not a great deal. Miss Keith insists upon keeping her horse ahead of mine. It is snowing! Did you know it?"

Dorothea jumped up and ran to the window. "It wasn't just now when I looked out. Yes, it is." She peered through the pane, pressing her nose close to it. "It hasn't snowed since that first week you came, Cousin Claudia, and that's nearly a month ago. I hope it will snow fifty feet deep, so the cars can't run, and that the river will freeze so the boats can't go down it, and then you will have to stay;

and so would we, and we could all be together Christmas. Don't you wish so, too,
Uncle Winthrop?" She came back and leaned
against her uncle's chair. "Did you know
Cousin Claudia was going home next week?"

"She told me so this afternoon."

"I certainly am." Elbows on her knees and
chin in her hands, Claudia looked straight into
the fire. "If your wish comes true, Dorothea,
I'll get an air-ship. I expected to stay three
weeks, and will have stayed five before I get
back. I ought to be home this minute."

"I don't think five weeks is long. I think
it's very short." Dorothea took a seat on a
stool at her uncle's feet, and looked up in his
face. "Father says he thinks it's downright
mean in her to go before we do. Don't you
think she might stay, Uncle Winthrop?"

"I do." Laine changed his position and
looked away from Dorothea's eyes. "Is there
nothing we can do to make her change her
mind?"

"Is there?" Dorothea turned to Claudia.
"I think you ought to, for mother says Uncle
Winthrop is just beginning to act like a Chris-
tian in coming to see her regularly, and when
you go he might stop acting that way. Are

you going to stay to dinner to-night?" She
took Laine's hand and intertwined her fingers
in his. "Please do."

"In these clothes?"

Dorothea hesitated. "Mother wouldn't like
them, but—" She jumped up and clapped
her hands in excited delight. "Mother's got
a headache and isn't coming down to-night,
and if you will stay I think she will let me take
dinner with you. I hate foolishness about
clothes, and these are the becomingest ones
you wear; and, besides, at the Hunt Club you
eat in them, and why can't you do it here
just once? Wouldn't it be magnificent if I
could sit up?" Dorothea whirled round and
round. "Father is out of town, and Channing
has a tiny bit of cold and can't leave his room,
and I'm so lonesome. Oh, please, Uncle Winthrop, *please* stay!"

"Ask Miss Keith if I can stay. She may
have other engagements."

"Have you?" Dorothea was on her knees
by Claudia, hands on her shoulders. "And
may he stay? You won't have to change your
clothes, either. You look precious in those
riding things, and, when you take the coat off,
anybody who didn't know would think you

were a little girl, the skirt is so short and
skimpy; and your hair with a bow in the
back looks like me. Can't he stay, Cousin
Claudia?''

"If he wants to, of course. I'm sorry your
mother is sick. She didn't tell me at lunch."

"It's just a headache, and as father is away
and there was nothing to go to, I think she
thought she'd take a rest and read something.
Are you going out to-night?"

Claudia got up. "No, I'm not going out;
but I have a letter to write. Will you stay to
dinner, Mr. Laine?"

"I will. Thank you very much, Miss Warrick. The invitation was forced from Miss
Keith, but I accept it notwithstanding."
Laine, who had risen, put his hand on Dorothea's shoulder. "I think we will have a very
nice dinner-party."

"I'll chaperone it!" Dorothea rose to full
height and balanced herself on her toes. "Miss
Robin French said she couldn't go on some
trip the other day because there was no chaperone; and if a lady with a mole on her chin
and nearly forty has to have a chaperone, I
guess you all will. Please don't stay long,
Cousin Claudia. If you don't want to see

mother, Uncle Winthrop, I'll talk to you, for
after dinner I will have to go right straight to
bed, being a brought-up-on-a-book child, and
then you and Cousin Claudia will be all by
yourselves. Maybe if you asked mother,
though, she might let me sit up just this once.
Shall I go and tell her you say so?"

Laine held the curtains for Claudia to pass
out. "We wouldn't be so cruel as to keep her
up, would we?" he asked, and smiled in the
eyes turned quickly from his. "You will not
be gone long, and you won't change your
dress?"

"I will be back in time for dinner—and I
won't change my dress. Tell Dorothea about
the birds we saw this afternoon."

During the hour that passed before Claudia
came back Dorothea had a chance that seldom came for uninterrupted conversation, and
that her uncle said little was not noticed for
some time. Presently she looked up.

"I don't believe you've opened your lips
since Cousin Claudia went up-stairs," she said.
"I don't wonder you don't know where you
went this afternoon if you didn't see any more
than you're hearing now. You don't know a
thing I've been talking about."

Laine raised his head with a start. "Oh yes, I do. You were saying—saying—"

"I told you so! You didn't even know where you were! You were way off somewhere." Dorothea's voice was triumphant. "I want to ask you something, Uncle Winthrop. I won't tell anybody." She settled herself more comfortably on the stool at his feet, and crossed her arms on his knees. "Don't you think my Cousin Claudia is nice?"

"Very nice." Laine took out his handkerchief, wiped his glasses, and held them to the light.

"And don't you think she has a lovely mouth? When she talks I watch her like I haven't got a bit of sense." Dorothea scanned her uncle's face critically. "Your eyes are dark; and hers are light, with dark rims around the seeing part, and she just comes to your shoulder; but you look so nice together. I hope you feel sorry about the things you said about her before she came."

"What things?"

"That maybe her face was red and her hair was red and her hands were red, or if they weren't, maybe they were blue. Aren't you sorry?"

6

"Very sorry, Dorothea. I was rude and tired and worried that evening. Let's forget it."

"I never have told her, but I supposed you must have changed your mind, for you've been here so much lately, and gone to so many places with her that you don't like to go to, that I thought—"

"Thought what, Dorothea?"

"That maybe—" Dorothea stroked Laine's fingers one by one—"maybe you liked her a little bit. Don't you remember I asked you please to like her, and you didn't seem to think you would. But you do, don't you? I won't tell anybody. Don't you like her, Uncle Winthrop?"

"I like her very much, Dorothea." Into Laine's clear-cut face the color crept to his temples. "She is very different from any one I've—"

"I knew you would." Dorothea's hands came together excitedly. "I knew it the minute I saw her, for she isn't a bit frilly, and you don't like frills any more than I do, and she doesn't, either. She's sees through people like they were glass, and she tells us the grandest, shiveringest, funniest stories you ever heard.

I bet she's telling Channing one this minute. She loves children. I'm so glad you like her, Uncle Winthrop. I knew you would if you saw her, but I didn't know you'd see her so much."

"How could I help it if I saw her once? The trouble has been to get her to see me. Perhaps she thinks I am too old to—"

"Oh, she knows you aren't the sweetheart kind—Miss Robin French told her so, and mother and everybody says you are too set in your ways to get married, and that's why I think she likes you, because you aren't that sort. She hates flum talk, and you talk sense and things. She told father so. Here she is now. Please stay with Uncle Winthrop, Cousin Claudia, while I ask mother if I may take dinner with you." Dorothea got up. "You took off your riding boots, didn't you?"

Claudia looked at her slippers. "I surely did. I never wear high shoes in the house. Your mother says you may take dinner with us, but she wants to see you as soon as it is over. Her headache is better, but she doesn't feel like coming down to-night."

X

A DISCOVERY

IN a chair of curious carving, his feet on a pile of books which had been unpacked, but for which there was as yet no place, Winthrop Laine leaned back, partly relaxed, partly tense, and with half-shut eyes looked at a picture on the wall opposite. For an hour, two hours, he had sat like this. On his desk was an unfinished article, but "The Punishments of Progress" did not interest to-night, and after vain effort to write he had thrown the pages aside and yielded to the unrest which possessed him.

In his hands was a small calendar, and with it he tapped unconsciously the arm of his chair; but after a while he again looked at it and with his pencil marked the date of the month. It was the fifteenth of December. Miss Keith was going home on the eighteenth. Three days of her visit yet remained, a month of it had passed, and after she went— He stirred uneasily, changed his position, put down the calendar, then got up and began to walk the length of the room backward and forward. A long mirror filled the space between the two southern windows, and for some time as he reached it he avoided the face seen therein; but after a while he stopped in front of it, hands in his pockets, and spoke with smiling bitterness to it.

"Take it off, man, take it off! All men wear masks, but they needn't go to bed with them. For years you've pretended, smiled, sworn, played with all the toys, worked with the best you had, and believed you were content. And you're finding out at forty what a fool you've been. You love her. She isn't married yet, if she is engaged to another man— and if you've no fight in you, go make a hole and get in it!"

In the glass he saw his face whiten, saw the lines on his forehead swell, saw his eyes grow dark with rebellious pain, and, turning away, went to a window, opened it, and let the cold air blow upon him. Few people were on the street, and in the windows opposite was little light. The neighborhood was exclusively correct; and only that evening walking home from the club the man with him had frankly envied his manner of life, his freedom and independence. He closed the window, turned off some of the lights, and went back to his chair. "I am an entirely free and independent person," he said aloud. "A most desirable condition for a man without a heart." Why did men have hearts, anyhow, and especially such a queer kind as he had. In the days of his youth he had expected the days of his maturity to find him married, find him with the responsibilities and obligations of other men; but he had strange views of marriage. One by one his friends had entered the estate; he had helped them enter it, but he had acquired an unhealthy habit of watching their venture with wonder at its undertaking and with doubt of its success, and the years had gone by with no desire on his part to assume the risk. What he saw was not the life he wanted. Just what he did want he was not sure; but years of contact with much that blights and withers had not killed his belief in certain old-fashioned things, and if they could not come true the journey would be made alone.

What whimsical ways fate had of deciding

great issues. Four weeks ago he was something of a piece of mechanism, fairly content with his drab-colored life; and now a girl had entered it and brought to him visions too fair and beautiful to be viewed unveiled, and he knew at last the mystery and power of love. Almost a week of her stay had gone before he met her. In those that followed, he had seen her many times, but frequently he had to stand back and know that others were taking her time when there was none for him to lose.

Should love come to him, he had imagined he would pursue it with the same directness and persistence which had impelled the securing of whatever was determined upon, and instead he was that most despicable of things — a coward.

She was so young—fourteen years younger than he—and what was his to offer in exchange for her life of varied interests, of sweet, sane, helpful, happy things of which he knew so little? He had thought he knew life, its all sides; and unknown to herself she had shown him what had not been understood before, and his was cold and colorless by the side of the warmth and glow of hers.

Yesterday he had known, however, he would not wait long. After she had returned to her

home he would go to it and tell her why he had
come. All through the day certain words had
sung in his ears, and over his books had danced
and blurred the figures he was making; and
before him in fancy she was waiting for his
coming when the day was done, was in the
room with outstretched hands to give him
greeting as he entered the door. The light of a
new vision had blinded, and in its fire the loneliness of his life had stood out in chill clearness,
and no longer could it be endured. Some one
to care if the days were dark, some one to share
the giving and taking of life. At the thought
of trust so sacred, his face had whitened, and in
his heart unconscious prayer had sprung.

That was yesterday. This afternoon he had
stopped at his sister's home for tea, as he had
done for days past now, and, Dorothea being
sick, he had gone up to see her and give her the
book bought for her. As usual, she had much
to say, and he let her talk uninterruptedly. It
was of Claudia that she talked, always of
Claudia, and he had listened in a silence that
gave chance for much detail.

"She gets more letters!" Dorothea's hands
came together as if very full. "Every day
there is one from the same person, sometimes

A DISCOVERY

two, and specials and telegrams; and sometimes he talks over the telephone. I know his handwriting now. She lets me come in her room whenever I want to. I don't see how one person could have so much to say. I knew he must be her sweetheart, and I asked mother, and mother says she's engaged to a man in Washington. Miss Robin French told her. Mother thinks it's real strange Claudia didn't tell her.'' And he had answered nothing, but had gone down the steps and out of the house, and to no one said good night.

XI

A CHANCE ENCOUNTER

LAUDIA glanced at the clock. She must be dressed by seven. Hurriedly she put aside the letters which could wait, and began to write.

"Just three days more, precious mother, and I will leave for home. I've seen such remarkable things; heard such wonderful music; been to so many parties and luncheons and teas and dinners; met so many people, some fearfully, dreadfully dressed, some beautifully, gorgeously gowned, that my brain is a plum-pudding, and my mind mere moving pictures. It's been a lovely visit. Channing is a dear, and Hope has done her full duty, but it's something of a strain to dwell in the tents of the wealthy. I'm so glad we're not wealthy, mother. There are hundreds of things I'd like money for, but I've gotten to be as afraid of it as I am of potato-bugs when the plants are well up. It has a way of making you think things

82

A CHANCE ENCOUNTER

that aren't so.   I do hope Uncle Bushrod's cold is better.

"I've tried to fill all the orders from everybody, but some I haven't found yet.   Hope and her friends shop only in the expensive stores, and the prices are so paralyzing that, though outwardly I don't blink, I'm inwardly appalled; but I put the things aside as if undecided whether to get them or something nicer.   I'm afraid I don't mean I'm glad we're not wealthy. Certainly when shopping I don't wish it.   I want millions then.   Millions!   And when I get among the books I'd like to be a billionaire. To-morrow I'm going out by myself and finish up everything.   Hope would be horrified at my purchases, for Hope has forgotten when she, too, had to be careful in her expenditures. Her brother hasn't.

"Did I tell you about the crazy mistake I made?   I thought, from what Dorothea told me, he was an old gentleman, her mother's uncle, and wrote him a note before I met him. Dorothea adores him, and when his dog died I was so sorry I told him so.   I wonder what does make me do such impulsive things!   I get so discouraged about myself.   I'll never, never be a proper person.   He isn't old.

83

"I wish you could see the letter Beverly wrote me from Mammy Malaprop. She says she is 'numberating the date of my return to the dissolute land in which I live, and is a-preparing to serve for supper all the indelicacies of the season.' If I didn't know old Malaprop I'd think Beverly was making up her messages, but no imagination could conceive of her twists and turns of the English language.

"Are the hens laying at all? and please tell Andrews to watch the sheep carefully; it's so bitterly cold.

"I've had a beautiful time, but, oh, mother dear, I shall be so glad to get home, where there are real things to do and where you all love me just for myself! Every night I kiss your picture and wish it was you. Best love for everybody. I have Gabriel's little trumpet.

"Devotedly,
"CLAUDIA.

"*P. S.*—We are going again to-night to the opera. If only you were going, too! I never see anything beautiful, hear anything beautiful, that I don't wish you could see it and hear it also. I'm so glad I brought my riding-habit. They have been the best things of all, the long,

A CHANCE ENCOUNTER

splendid rides in the country. So much nicer
than motoring. Mr. Laine rides better than
any city man I know. Three days more and I
leave for home.

"C."

Guilty gladness at being alone, at getting off
by herself and going where she chose, so possessed her the next day that as Claudia passed
Mrs. Warrick's sitting-room she tip-toed lest
she be called in and a moment of her precious
freedom be lost. Several hours of daylight were
still left, but there was much to be done; and
hurriedly she went down the steps, hurriedly
walked to the avenue, and caught the 'bus she
saw coming with a sigh of thankfulness. In the
center of the shopping district she got out and
disappeared soon after in one of the stores.
It was her only chance for the simple purchases
to be made for the slim purses of her country
friends; and as she read first one list and then
the other she smiled at the variety of human
desires and the diversities of human needs, and
quickly made decisions. A letter received just
before leaving the house had not been read, but
its writing was recognized, and going to the
door she tried to make out the scrawly con-

85

tents and get, at the same time, the breath of
fresh air brought in by its opening as hurrying
customers came and went. To read there was
impossible, however. Darkness had fallen; and,
going outside for a moment, she looked up and
down at the surging, pushing, shivering crowd
and wondered as to the time. She was not
through, and she must finish before going back.

"Is Madame Santa Claus ready to go home?"

Startled, she looked up. "Oh, Mr. Laine,
I'm so glad! Indeed I'm not through, and it's
dark already. Do you think Hope will mind
if I don't get back for tea?"

"I think not." He smiled in the troubled
face. "What is left to be done?"

"This among other things." Together they
moved slowly down the crowded street, and she
held the letter in her hand toward him. "It's
from Mrs. Prosser, who has eleven children and
a husband who is their father and that's all.
They live on faith and the neighbors, but she
has sold a pig and sent me part of the money
with which to buy everybody in the family a
Christmas present. That's all I've made out."

Laine took the sheets of paper torn from a
blank-book and looked at them under an
electric light. "This Syro-Phœnician writing

needs what it can't get out here," he said, after
a half-minute's pause. "A cipher requires a
code, and a code means sitting down. Aren't
you cold? You are. Come over here and
we'll have some tea and work it out together."
And before protest could be made they were in
a hotel across the street and at a table on which
a shaded light permitted a closer examination
of the penciled scrawl which went for writing.
Slowly he read aloud:

"DERE MISS CLAUDIA,—The chillern is near
bout set me crazy sence I tole 'em I was agoin'
to ask you to do me some favors which is to
buy for me some New York krismus presents.
I have sole the pig and I am a-puttin' in this
six dollars and sixteen cents. I would have
sent seven dollars even but the baby had the
colic so bad I had to git some more of that
pain - killer which I give the hoss onct, and
Johnnie lost the change comin' home from the
store. The baby is well, but the hoss ain't.
The followin' is what I would like to have.
Ifen you can't git the things, git what you can.
I have confidence in your jedgment.

"2 pare sox and a maresharm pipe for the
old man. Don't spend more than fifty cents
on him. He drunk up the whiskey your ma

give me for the mincemeat for Thanksgivin'
and I had to lock him up in the garret. He'd
like the pipe yaller.

"1 A blew skarf pin—Johnnie.

"2 A bracelet. Bras will do if you can't git
gold. Minnie is the meekest and don't look
for much but she wants a bracelet awful bad.

"3 A box of paper and envellopes for Maizzie
—Maizzie's got a bow. He lives in the next
county. I don't let the chillern say nothin'.
I'm 'fraid they'll scare the ducks.

"4 A wax doll in pink tarlton for Rosy. She
won't be here next krismus. The doctor done
tole me, and my hart it have been hurtin' so
ever since that I have to hide every now and
then so as to git my breath good. Sometimes
I can't help chokin', I can't. She seen a doll
in pink tarlton onct and the other night I
heard her talkin' up the chimney and she was
askin' Santa Claus to bring her one if he could
spare it. Ifen you can't git all the things with
the pig money, please'm git the doll, and in
pink, please'm, and let the others go."

Laine took up his cup of tea and drank it
slowly. "Part of this is hard to make out,"
he said, after a moment. "I can't see it very
well."

A CHANCE ENCOUNTER

"All of it is hard." Claudia put a piece of cracker in her mouth. "But it's a wonder she can write at all. The boys are as trifling as their father, and she does the work of five people. Is that all?"

Laine began again. "Becky say she don't want nothin' but a pare of silk stockings. She's crazy, but she seen the summer girls with 'em and I don't reckon it will do no harm if we ain't pracktical at krismus. It do seem like krismus ain't for prackticals. 40 cents is her share.

"Sam he wants a harmonicum, and Bobbie he just set his hart on a sled. I don't reckon you can get that in your trunk, and ifen you can't a necktie will have to do. The other chillern is so small it don't make no difference what you get for them, any little thing you can pick up will please 'em. They is all so excited about havin' presents from New York that they's plum crazy. I don't know what the county would do without you, Miss Claudia. You is everybody's friend and everybody is—"

Claudia put out her hand. "Oh, that part doesn't matter. I'll take it now. We'll have to go. Are you ready?"

"Not quite." Laine, who had finished the let-

ter, handed it to her, then took out a note-book
and pencil. "Are you sure you can remember the things? Hadn't I better write them
down?"

Claudia shook her head. "Not a bit of use.
These are the last to get, and then I'm through.
Are you?"

"Am I what?"

"Through."

"Through what?"

"With your Christmas things. I don't suppose men have as much to do as women and
don't have to begin so early. Some people
don't love Christmas. It's such a pity."

"It's a pity the old Christmas has given way
to the new one. With many it's a sort of hold-
up. I don't believe in it."

Claudia's arms were folded on the table, and
her eyes were gravely looking into his. "What
kind do you believe in?"

Into Laine's face the color crept slowly, then
he laughed. "I really don't know. I only
know the present kind is wrong."

"You know a great many things that are
wrong, don't you?"

"I'm afraid I do." With his handkerchief
Laine wiped his glasses, put them back, and

90

again tapped the table. "That is, I know a great many things that aren't nice to know."

"Most of us do. It isn't difficult to see what isn't nice in people or things." She got up. "I'm sorry you don't love Christmas."

"Why should I love it? For the men at the office there are checks; for my brother's widow and children are other checks; for Hope, another. A man makes a mess of buying presents. Cigars for men and flowers for women are the two orders telephoned in advance for the few so remembered. The employees at the clubs, the servants at the house, the—the associations which do things merely mean more money, and money—"

"I think I should hate Christmas, too, if it merely meant the writing of checks or the giving of gold. I wouldn't want a million if there was no love with it." Eyes on her muff, she smoothed it softly. "That is what Christmas is for. To take time to remember, and to let people know we do care—and to make somebody glad. Let me see." On her fingers she enumerated the things desired by Mrs. Prosser. "Harmonicum, silk stockings, socks, yellow pipe, blue scarf-pin, bracelet (brass or gold), box of paper, sled, and—"

"A doll in pink tarleton." Again in Laine's face the color crept slowly. He hesitated. "In all my life I never bought a doll or a sled or anything except books for children. May I go with you? And would—would you mind if I got that doll?"

XII

CHRISTMAS SHOPPING

IVE minutes later Laine and Claudia were caught in the crowd of Christmas shoppers and valiantly made their way to a counter on which were objects gay and glittering. With a seriousness and persistency that was comic to the girl watching him, Laine began with the blue scarf-pin and the bracelet, but not until he was giving an order did she touch him on the arm and draw him aside.

"We can't get those, Mr. Laine, indeed we can't." She nodded in the direction of the counter. "There aren't but six dollars and sixteen cents of the pig money, and a dozen things to buy yet."

"Oh, blow the pig money! She won't know the difference. That pin is only one dollar and ninety-eight cents and the bracelet two dollars and forty-eight cents. Nothing could be worse than that, could it?"

93

"It could. Johnnie is a lazy good-for-nothing, and twenty-five cents is all his pin is to cost. It will be big and blue, but not a penny over twenty-five can be spent on it. I think we'd better get the doll and the silk stockings and the sled first. I've already bought a doll for Rosy, but it's in white, and we'll have to get the pink one."

"And is the pig money going to do all that?" Laine's eyes were searching Claudia's.

"It is." She laughed and turned away as if to see some one who was passing. "It doesn't matter whose pig."

"Then I'll play the pig to-night! I've played it the wrong way often enough. Why can't we be sensible? I've got a spending jag on, and I've never been Christmas shopping before. Something is happening to my backbone, something that used to happen in the days when I hung up my stocking. Please be good and let me have a little Christmas!"

Claudia's forehead wrinkled and for a moment she hesitated, then again her eyes sought his doubtfully. "I don't know whether I ought to. You are very kind, but—"

"But nothing. I'm merely very selfish. Those things are all right. Come on and let's

94

go in the toy department. The doll is the most
important of all, and don't dolls have carriages
or something? Here, this way to the elevator."

To the joy of it, the surrender to inherent
instinct, to the child that is dormant in all,
Claudia and Laine yielded, went in and out
among the sea of toys, and critically doll after
doll was examined, compared, laid down and
taken up, and finally decided upon; and as
Laine gave the address he looked at Claudia
for final confirmation and approval.

"You're sure it's pink? Her mother said
pink, you know."

"Pink! It's the pinkest pink I ever saw.
It is much too grand. But, oh, those patient
little eyes! I didn't think she'd be here this
Christmas. You will make her so happy, Mr.
Laine."

"Not I." He shook his head. "It is you.
What does a man know about things like this?
But what else does she want? I never had any
opinion of a one-piece Santa Claus. These
things would make a monk want children of
his own. How about those youngsters that
anything will please? and don't you have to
have things for stockings?"

With hurried decisions, as if afraid he might
95

not be allowed to do what he chose, Laine went up and down and in and out among the many sections into which the department was divided, and made his selections with entire disregard of appropriateness; and Claudia, keeping near, countermanded with equal firmness all that was unwise. So warm at times did their dissensions wax that the sales-girl following would smile and point out something before unseen, hoping a mutual surrender would accept the compromise, and presently she brought up a cash register and held it toward Laine.

"Most children like these," she said, "and as your wife doesn't care for the mechanical toys—"

Laine turned away. With pitiless reality the play of it all came over him, and he walked off lest the sudden surging of his blood be heard.

"But I'm not his wife." Claudia's voice was cool and even. "He doesn't know the children he is getting these things for, and I do. But Channing would like this register, Mr. Laine. And Dorothea told me she wanted a drawing-table like that one over there. Have you bought Dorothea's present yet?"

Laine came back. "Only books. Her mother gets the other things for me. If she'd like that, get it."

Out of his voice had gone all spirit, and Claudia, noticing, looked up. "You're tired, aren't you? I think we'd better stop."

Laine laughed. "Tired? No, I'm not tired. I'm having a great time. Playing make-believe is a good game. I haven't played it lately, and I was doing it rather hard. I wonder what that bunch of people are over there for? A number of children seem to be among them."

The girl waiting on them looked around. It was Santa Claus, she explained, who was taking the names and addresses, with a list of the presents most wanted by the children who were there to tell where they lived. "Some of them have been here all day. That little lame fellow was among the first to come, and Santa Claus hasn't seen him yet. The crowd pushes him out so, and there's no one to lift him up high enough to be seen. He's held that piece of paper in his hand for hours."

Laine looked closer. On the outskirts of the crowd, his thin little face still eagerly trying to peer between the shifting circles, his crutches held tightly by hands too thin to grasp them properly, he saw the boy pointed out by the girl, and, without a word, he walked toward

97

him. As he drew nearer, the head of Santa Claus could be seen over those of the crowd, but to the child he was still invisible; and as Laine saw the pinched face he swore softly under his breath.

For half a minute he stood by the boy's side, then touched him on the shoulder. "What is it, son? Can't you make the old fellow see you?"

The child shook his head. "Somebody always gets in ahead. I ain't tall enough."

"Here, hold your crutches." With a swift movement Laine swung the boy on his shoulders. "There, can you see him all right?"

"Yes, sir. And he can see me!" The thin little hand was held up, and Laine felt the quiver that ran over the frail body. "He sees me!"

"Well, my man"—Santa Claus was noticing at last—"what is it that you want?"

"A coat for mother. Black, please." Soft and eager the words came quickly. "And a worsted skirt, and some shoes for Dick, and a muff for Katie."

"Oh, I'm not bringing anything but toys this time. Only toys. Quick, what are they?"

On his shoulders again Laine felt a quiver,

this time of sudden relaxation, and heard a sob
that was quickly smothered. "Oh, I don't
need toys, and mother hasn't got a piece of
coat."

Laine coughed and caught the eye of Santa
Claus, and by telepathy made the latter understand his questions must continue. Two
minutes and they were over, the child's name
and address taken, his desires made known, and
as he put him down on the floor Laine took
from the trembling fingers the piece of paper
which for hours had been tightly held and put it
in his pocket.

"All right, son." He slipped some money in
his hand. "Run down-stairs and get something to eat before you go home, and don't
worry about the things—they'll be there
Christmas, Scoot!" And with a pat Laine sent
him off.

Coming back he turned to Claudia. "Are
you through up here? The yellow pipe and
the socks for the man who gets locked in the
garret are down-stairs, I suppose."

For answer Claudia looked in his face as if
not hearing. "Merciful goodness!" she said.
"I had forgotten all about this being Tuesday!
I ought to be home this minute. A friend from

99

692712 A

Washington is coming to dinner to-night. What time is it?"

Laine looked at his watch. "A friend from Washington" was what he read. He turned the face toward her. "What is it? I can't see it in this light."

"Seven-twenty-five!" Claudia sat down dejectedly. "You don't suppose they could be waiting, do you?"

"I don't.' Laine smiled a twisted little smile. "Channing by nature is a train-despatcher. Dinner on the dot and served swiftly is his one household demand. They will be half through before we can get there."

"And I'm starving." She got up. "Well, I can't help it. I had no business forgetting, but I'm always doing things I oughtn't."

"We'll go up to Sherry's. Dinner isn't limited to Hope's house. I'll telephone and explain."

"Oh, I mustn't! It isn't just dinner. I have an engagement. Do you think we could get there very quickly? I can't understand how I forgot!"

XIII

"DID you ring, sir?"

Moses, standing at the door, waited, and as he waited he talked to himself. "Something is the matter with Mr. Laine. He ain't never call Gineral's name since he done pass away, and I know the miss of him has been a-smartin', but don't seem like that would have made him so restless like he been. 'Tain't like him to come in and go right out, and come back and go out again. He got something on his mind, a kind of warfare like." He coughed slightly and again spoke. "Did you ring, Mr. Laine?"

"I did. Five minutes ago. As a member of the leisure class you'd take a blue ribbon, Moses. Where in the devil are you? Why don't you come in? I can't talk to air."

"I was waitin' to see if I was mistook about the bell." Moses came inside the room.

"Where I come from folks don't step so lively as they do up here, and old Colonel Tayloes, he used to say there ain't nothin' so inelegant as hurry, lessen 'tis worry. But of course I shouldn't have had no discussion in my mind about that bell. I got a bad way of projectin' when—"

"You don't want to move. You have. Any day an affidavit is needed to that effect I'll sign it. Did you go to that address I gave you yesterday?"

"Yes, sir. I went and I been a-tryin' to forget I went ever since I got back. It's God's truth the boy told you. I seen him and his ma, and all the other children 'cept those at work, and the whole of 'em was livin' in two rooms, and a closet where the biggest boy slept. Their pa he got kilt at the shops where he work, and the lawyer what undertook to get damages got 'em, and they ain't seen him since."

"Did you notice the size of the woman and the age of the children?"

"Yes, sir. The mother she come near 'bout up to my shoulder and was thin and wore-out lookin'. The two little ones was four and two years old. You saw the lame one. There's a girl seven. She's a puller-out of bastin's, her ma said, and the oldest girl is fourteen. She's a runner, or a cash, or somethin' in a store. The biggest boy is in a foundry-shop and the lame one sells papers."

"A mother and six children." Laine made some notes in a book and put it back in his pocket. "I'm going out. Have a cab here at eight-thirty. The things I bring back will be put in the room at the end of the hall. On Christmas Eve you are to buy what I've mentioned in this"—he handed him an envelope— "and with them take the bundles in the room to the place you went to yesterday. You are not to know who sent them, and when you come back you are to forget you've been, and no one is to be told. You have a great habit of telling Dorothea things. I'm understood, am I?"

"Yes, sir. You is understood. I know about a left hand and a right hand. God knows I'll be glad to go again if it's to take some Christmas to them. That woman's face kinder hant me ever sence I seen it. 'Twasn't mad or nothin', but plum beat out. I had to make a little egg-nog for my stomach when I got home. 'Tain't time for egg-nog, but a disturbance in the stomach—"

103

"You're having a disturbance in your stomach too often. Get that cab, will you, and tell them to hurry."

Two hours later he was back. No doubt he had done foolishly, bought unwisely; but there had been no time for indecision, and the woman who waited on him had been a great help. As he was shown warm dresses and thick coats for the mother and little girls, suits and shoes and stockings for the boys, bedclothing, towels, soap, ribbons, and neckties, he had smiled at the absurdity of his opinion being asked concerning things of which he was as ignorant as a blind baby; but with determination he kept on until the woman told him he had gotten enough. With the toys he was more confident; and, remembering Claudia's restrictions, he had exercised what he believed was excellent judgment and only bought what was probably appropriate.

When the bed in the end room had been piled with his purchases, the door locked, and the key in Moses's pocket, Laine went into the library, turned off its brilliant lights, and, leaving only the lamp burning, closed the door, sat down in his high-back chair, and lighted a cigar. After the stir and glow of the store the silence

of the room was oppressive, its emptiness
chilled, and, unthinking, he put his hand down
by the side of his chair and flipped his fingers
as he was wont to do when calling General.
With an indrawn breath he drew his hand back
and put it in his pocket. His Christmas
shopping was over. A very unexpected Christmas shopping it had been. In all that city of
millions there were few personal purchases to
be made for others. What had to be gotten
Hope got. Not since the death of his mother
had Christmas meant more than something to
be dreaded and endured. And to Claudia it
meant so much.

Why had she come into his life? Why was
hers the divine gift of recognition which dis-
pensed with the formal development of friend-
ship and yielded, as a flower its fragrance, the
warmth and gladness, the surety and genuine-
ness, that so long he had looked for. Apparently she was as unconscious as Dorothea, and
yet too many men had loved her for her not to
understand. Not by the subtlest sign had she
shown, however. Indifference or dislike would
have been more encouraging, but her cordial
frankness had been that of unstirred depths.

Suppose she was engaged to another man?

Was that any reason why he should not tell her of his love, ask her to be his wife? Puritanic scruples such as his were beyond pardon. A sense of honor might go too far. Why didn't he find out if it were true what Dorothea had told him? God! To have had a vision, only to go through life in darkness!

An hundred times in fancy he had heard the sweep of her skirts, the sound of her footsteps, the tones of her voice, and laughter gay and sweet and soft; an hundred times had seen the glad eyes grow grave, the forehead wrinkle in fine folds, the quick turn of her head; an hundred times had felt the touch of her hands; and he had never asked Hope to bring her to his home, lest her spirit should not come again.

The badinage of other days came to him, the days when women had rather bothered. They would be amused, these women, did they know his surrender to the god unknown at that time —the god he had sometimes smiled at because he had not known. Day after to-morrow she was going home. He had not seen her since the afternoon they had been shopping together. The man from Washington had claimed her time, and he had stayed away. Who was this man? To ask Hope or Channing had been impossible. Dorothea would be delighted to tell him. The instincts of her sex were well developed in Dorothea; and she missed no chance of letting him know of Claudia's engagements, of what she did, and where she went, and from whom her flowers came. Doubtless she would be delighted to tell him even more.

He got up and began to walk the length and breadth of the room. The sound of his footsteps was lost in the heavy rugs, and only the ticking of the clock broke the stillness, and presently it struck the hour of midnight. He took out his watch and looked at it. "Tomorrow she is going home," he said.

XIV

AN INFORMAL VISIT

T the door of what was still called the nursery Laine stood a moment, hesitating whether to go in or to go away. In a low rocking-chair Claudia was holding Channing, half-asleep in her arms; and at her feet Dorothea, on a footstool, elbows on knees and chin in the palms of her hands, was listening so intently to the story being told that for half a minute his presence was not noted.

Presently she looked up and saw him. "Come in." Her voice was a high whisper. "It's the grandest story. Wait a minute, Cousin Claudia." She ran toward the door and drew him in. "You'll have to stay with us," she said, "because mother and father have gone out. Some kind of a relation is in town and they had to go. Channing's got an awful cold, and mother said he could have anything he wanted, and he took Cousin Claudia to tell him stories. She's been doing it ever since dinner. He's asleep now, but—"

"I'm not asleep." Channing's eyes opened blinkingly. "She said they found the squirrel in a hollow down by the chestnut-tree, and the moonlight on the snow—the moonlight—on— the—snow." His head fell back on Claudia's bosom and, with a smile, she nodded to Laine and held out her hand.

"The spirit is valiant, but the flesh prevails. I'm so sorry Hope and Channing are out."

"I'm not." He drew a cushioned wicker chair close to the fire. "It's been long since I heard a good fairy story. Please don't stop."

Dorothea pushed the stool aside and settled herself comfortably in her uncle's lap. "It isn't a fairy story. You don't tell fairy stories at Christmas; they're for summer, when the windows are open and they can hide in the flowers and ride on the wind—the fairies, I mean —but this is Christmas." She twisted herself into a knot of quivering joy and hugged her arms with rapturous intensity. "It's all in my bones, and I'm nothing but shivers. Isn't it grand to have Christmas in your bones? Have you got it in yours?" She held Laine's face between her hands and looked at it anxiously. "Cousin Claudia has it in hers. She and I are just alike. We've been filling stockings to-day for some children Timkins told us about. They live near him, and their mother is sick and their father is dead, and they haven't a bit of money. Channing and I are going to hang our stockings up here before we go to grandmother's, and we're going to hang them up there again. I wish we were going to Cousin Claudia's. Of course, I love to go to grandmother's, but she lives in town and they don't have snow in Savannah; and at Cousin Claudia's they have everything. I mean everything Christmasy like I like. She's been telling us about when she was a little girl."

Dorothea's feet twisted around each other and her hands were laid palm to palm as her body swayed backward and forward in rhythmic movement. "They go out in the woods and cut cart-loads of holly and mistletoe and pine and Christmas-trees, and dress the house, and the fires roar up all the chimneys, and they kill the pigs—"

Channing sat upright and rubbed his eyes. "They don't kill the pigs at Christmas. She said they kill them when the persimmons get ripe."

"Well, they're killed and you eat them Christmas. They put a little one on the table with an apple in its mouth. And they pick out the fattest turkeys and ducks and geese and chickens; and they go to the smoke-house and punch and poke the hams and things; and the oysters come from the river; and Mammy Malaprop comes up from the gate, where she lives now, and helps make the cakes and the pies and plum-puddings and beaten biscuits; and Cousin Claudia says when she was a little girl Mammy Malaprop always gave her some of the Christmas cake to bake in egg-shells. I wish I could see somebody make a cake. And Christmas Eve they make egg-nog, and Uncle Bushrod makes the apple toddy two weeks before." She turned to her uncle. "Why don't you go down there, Uncle Winthrop? I bet you'd get Christmas in your bones if you did."

"I am very sure of it." Laine fixed Dorothea more firmly on his lap. "There is only one reason in the world why I don't go."

"What's that? We're going away, and you will be all alone if you don't. Can't he come, Cousin Claudia? He'd love it. I know he would."

THE MAN IN LONELY LAND

"I don't." Claudia moved her chair farther
from the firelight. "Christmas at Elmwood
would be punishment for a city man. We
are much too primitive and old-fashioned. He
would prefer New York."

"Would you?" Dorothea's arms were around
her uncle's neck, and her head nodded at his.
"Would you?"

"I would not." Laine's voice was a little
queer. "The punishment is all at this end.
I would rather spend Christmas at Elmwood
than anywhere on earth. But your Cousin
Claudia will not let me, Dorothea."

"Won't you really?" Dorothea slipped from
his lap, and, with hands on the arms of Claudia's
chair, gazed anxiously in her eyes. "He'll be
all alone if you don't. Please ask him, Cousin
Claudia! You said yourself there was always
so much company at Elmwood that one more
never mattered and you managed to put them
somewhere. Please—oh, *please* ask him, Cousin
Claudia!"

Claudia kissed the lips held close to her own.
"I think it is time for you to be in bed, Dorothea.
You are making your uncle say things he doesn't
mean. He can come to Elmwood if he wishes,
but—"

112

AN INFORMAL VISIT

Dorothea sprang back and, with arms extended and fingers flipping, danced round and round the room. "How magnificent! Now I won't have a thing on my mind!" With a last whirl she jumped in Laine's lap and took his hands in hers. "That's the only thing I hated about Christmas, your being here all by yourself." She gave a deep breath. "And now you'll be in that heavenly place with Cousin Claudia. When I get big I'm going there and hunt by the light of the moon, and hear the darkies sing when they're having a party with possum and hoe-cake, and—" She sat upright. "Did you know Cousin Claudia was going home to-morrow?"

Laine nodded. Speech had suddenly left him. He did not know whether to take Dorothea in the next room and lock her up or hold her close to his heart. What had the child done and made Claudia do? Christmas at Elmwood! His blood surged thickly, and as Dorothea settled back in his arms he looked up and met Claudia's eyes.

"I'm so scrumptious happy I feel like I'm in heaven!" Dorothea wriggled in sleepy content. "Please finish that story you were telling when Uncle Winthrop came in, Cousin Claudia.

You had gotten to where the little boy and the
little girl were knocking at the door of the big
house with the wreaths in the windows, and it
was snowing. I couldn't sleep to save my life
if I didn't know whether they got in or not.
Please finish it."

Claudia hesitated, then, changing Channing's
position, finished the story and glanced at the
clock. "It is time for you to be in bed, Dorothea. I have some notes to write and some
packing to—"

"Just one more and that's all." Dorothea
cuddled closer. "It's so nice and home-y with
just us in here. Please don't make me go yet.
Tell Uncle Winthrop a story"—she blinked
bravely—"and then I'll go—to—bed."

Laine leaned back and turned off the light
from the lamp on the table behind him, and as
the firelight played on Claudia's soft, blue
dress, on the slippered feet tapping the stool
on which they rested, ran up to the open throat
and touched the brown hair, parted and
brushed back in simple fashion, he held Dorothea close lest words he must not speak be
spoken. Presently he looked toward her.

"I am waiting," he said. "Will you tell me
a story, Santa Claudia?"

AN INFORMAL VISIT

"A story?" Her eyes were watching the curling flames. "What kind shall I tell you? I do not know the kind you like."

"I would like any kind that you would tell me."

She leaned her head back against the cushioned chair, and again her lashes seemed to touch her cheek. For a moment the soft silence was unbroken, then she turned her face toward him.

"Very well," she said. "I will tell you a story. It will be about the man who did not know."

XV

THE MAN WHO DID NOT KNOW

NCE upon a time there was a man who had to make a journey. He did not want very much to make it; and, not knowing whether it was to be a long journey or a short one, he did not feel a great deal of interest in it. Still it had to be made, and at its end he was to find out whether he had been a good traveler or a bad one.

"For a long time he did not notice very closely the road he was on. He had been so busy getting ready, first at school, where he studied a great many books that he might be better prepared for traveling, and then in business, where money must be made to give him comfort and pleasure on the way, that he did not have time to look around very much; but after a while he saw that the road was getting very dull and dusty, that most of the flowers were faded and

the fruits were not sweet and the birds did not
sing as they had sung when first he started out.
˹ "A great many people had been traveling the
same way he had. Though they seemed to be
having a good time, he had soon seen that most
of it was make-believe, and that much of their
energy was spent in trying to find something to
play with, that they might forget what kind of
journey they were on. He did not like these
people very specially. He did not know any
others, however, and he had kept up with them
because they had started out together; but,
little by little, he had slipped away from them,
and after a while he found that he was walking
most of the time by himself. At first he did
not mind. The things his friends cared for and
talked about did not greatly interest him, and
then it was he began to remember that a good
many things he had been passing were ugly and
cruel, and bitter and unjust. He could not
understand why some should travel in luxurious
ease while others could hardly get along, their
burdens were so great; why some rode in carriages, and others, sick and hungry and tired and
cold, could never stop lest they die upon the
road; and why some sang and others wept.

"In groups and pairs, and sometimes one by

one, they passed him, and as they went by he would look into their faces to see why they were traveling; but, like him, they did not know, they only knew they must keep on. And then one day he saw he had come back to where his journey had begun. He had been on the road to Nowhere—the road that wound round and round."

"Just like travelers in the desert." Dorothea's eyes made effort to open, but sleepily they closed again. "Why didn't he ask somebody the way?"

"He didn't think any one knew. He was much wiser than most of the people who passed him. To many who seemed to be in need he had given money; he was very generous, very kind, and he gave freely; but he always turned his head away when he gave. He did not like to see suffering and sorrow; and with sin of certain sorts he had no sympathy, and so he would not look. But after a while he had to look.

"He was standing at the place from which he had started, and, to his surprise, he saw what he had never seen before. Out from its center led all sorts of roads that stretched beyond sight, and on each of them people were traveling, all kinds of people, and he knew he could no longer stand still. He must take one of these roads, but which one he did not know. As he stood uncertain what to do, he felt some one touch him; and, looking down, he saw a child; and into his strong hand the child slipped his little one.

"'I have been waiting for you,' he said. 'I have been waiting a long, long time.'

"'For me?' The man drew back. 'You can't have been waiting for me. I do not know you, child!'

"He heard a little sigh, as soft as the stir of wings, and again the boy smiled.

"'But I know you. There is much for you to do.'

"Again the man held back. 'There is nothing for me to do. I pay my taxes and give my tithes, and let the world alone.'

"'You cannot let the world alone. It is your world.' The boy looked up. 'Come, they are waiting.'

"'Who is waiting?'

"'Your people.'

"'I have no people. There is no one waiting for me.'

"The child shook his head. 'You do not know your people, and they are waiting. We must hurry, the time is short. We will go on this road first, and then on that, and then on that and that and that. On each one they are waiting.'

"All through the night they traveled, uphill and down, and in and out of narrow paths and hidden places, and everywhere he saw them, the people he had never known. Into the darkness of pits and mines, into the fires of foundries and furnaces, into the factories where wheels turned night and day, and into the holds of the ships of the sea, the child led him to show him the people who were his. In cellars and garrets, in jails and prisons, in shops and stores, in hunger and cold, in the silence of sickness, the noise of sin, they were waiting for his coming; and in their faces was that which made him cover his, and he begged the child to take him where breath could come again.

"But the child held his hand still tighter. 'You have traveled long and you have not known,' he said. 'You helped to make things as they are, and now you must see.'

"'I helped to make things as they are? I have not even dreamed such things could be!'

"'I know. And that is why I came. They are your people; and you did not know.'

"And then the child took him on another

road, one that was smooth and soft, and the air that blew over it was warm and fragrant. On it the women wore jewels and laces and gorgeous gowns; and men threw gold away to see it shine in the sunlight, threw it that others might see them throw.

"'Why do we come here?' the man asked. 'They are not waiting. They do not need.'

"The child looked up in his face. 'They, too, are waiting—for some one to let them know. And they, too, need, for hearts hurt everywhere. Sometimes the loneliest ones are here.'

"Before answer could be made, the main road was left, and in a tiny by-path they heard the laughter of children's voices; and, looking ahead, they saw a little house with wreaths in the windows through which the glow of fire-light sent threads of dancing light upon the snow, and the door was open.

"'We will go in,' said the child, 'for there is welcome.'

"Inside, the mother and the father and all the children were hanging holly on the walls and bringing bundles and boxes and queer-shaped packages from the other rooms and hiding them under chairs and tables and in out-of-the-way places; and presently a row of stockings was hung from the chimneypiece, and the children clapped their hands and danced round and round the room. And then they threw their arms around their father and mother and kissed them good night and left them that Kris Kringle might come in.

"'They have no money, but are very rich,' said the child. 'They love much.'

"Over long roads and short ones, over some that were dark and some that were bright, they went their way, and presently they came to a shabby, snow-covered street where children were pressing their faces against shop-windows, and men and women were hurrying in and out of crowded stores; and the child loosened his hold upon the man's hand. 'I must go now,' he said.

"'Oh no, you must not go!' Quickly the man reached for him. 'You must not go. I do not even know your name!'

"The child shook his head. 'I cannot stay. And some day you will know my name.'

"'But why did you come? If you must leave me, why did you come?'

"'Why did I come?' In the crowd he was slipping away, but the light in his face streamed through it. 'I came to bring Good-Will to men. I came that Men might Know.'"

XVI

A CHANGE OF PLANS

WHEN Moses saw Mr. Laine hurrying from one side of his bedroom to the other, opening bureau drawers and closet doors and throwing things on floor and bed in an excited haste never seen before, he was convinced that something was the matter with his master's mind. It had happened very suddenly. He had eaten his dinner, but eaten so little that Caddie, the cook, was in angry tears. For days her finest efforts had been ignored, and temptation after temptation, triumphs of skill on her part, had come back barely tasted, and, what was worse, with no comment made upon them. Praise had hitherto never been withheld, and to please him no labor was too great, no time too precious to be expended; but if this was what she was to get— Caddie was Irish, and she threw birds and sweetbreads in the slop-can and slammed the door in Moses's face.

"No, siree! I ain't a-goin' to let white folks' eatin's go in black folks' stomachs, that I ain't!" she said, and shook both fists up at the ceiling. "Pigs can have it first; there's some reason for pigs, but that nigger man Moses!" Her nose went up, her head went back, and she wept aloud. The work of her hands was as naught. She would die and be buried before Moses should have it!

At his coffee Laine had asked for his mail, asked it to get Moses out of the room. A creature who smiled always was not always to be endured, and to-night he was in no mood for smiles.

Moses brought two letters. "These is all," he said.

Laine waved him out and opened the top one, which was from Dorothea. What a queer propensity the child had for writing! Elbow on the table and cigar in hand, he began to read indifferently; but in a moment his hand stiffened and his face whitened to the lips, and, half aloud, he read it again.

DEAR UNCLE WINTHROP,—I forgot to tell you something the other night. I told you once that Cousin Claudia's sweetheart was that Washington man. He isn't. I asked her and she said he wasn't. I asked her if she was going to marry him and she said she was not. I don't like to say things that aren't true and that's why I'm telling you. Miss Robin French thinks she knows everything. We are going away to-morrow.

Your loving niece,

DOROTHEA.

P. S.—When a lady gets married she has to go away with a man, don't she? That's why she isn't going to get married. She says she loves Elmwood better than any kind of man she's seen yet. I'm so glad, aren't you?

D.

For half a moment longer Laine stared at the paper in his hand, then, with the cigar, it fell to the floor, and he lifted his head as if for breath. Something had snapped, something that had been tense and tight, and his throat seemed closing. Presently his face dropped in his arms. What a fool he had been! He had let the prattle of a child torture and torment him and keep him silent, and now she was gone. After a while he raised his head and wiped his hands, which were moist; and, as he saw the writing on the letter beside him, his heart gave a click so queer that he looked around to see if the door was shut. Quickly he opened the envelope and tried to read: he couldn't see; the words ran into each other, and, going over to a side light, he held the paper close to it.

125

THE MAN IN LONELY LAND

DEAR MR. LAINE,—Ours is a very old-fashioned, country Christmas, but we will be glad to have you spend it with us if you have not made other arrangements. Uncle Bushrod and I will be at the wharf Wednesday to meet the boat from Fredericksburg, and if you are on it we will bring you home with us, and if not we will be sorry, so come if you can. One or two other friends are coming that day, but most of our guests are here. All the trains from the North stop at Fredericksburg, and the boat that goes down the river leaves any time after 2 P.M., the hour of leaving depending upon the amount of freight, the convenience of the passengers, and the readiness of the captain. As there's a boat only three times a week you can't get here in time for Christmas unless you make the Tuesday boat which should reach Brooke Bank, that's our landing, by ten o'clock Wednesday morning. Do come if you can.

Sincerely,   CLAUDIA KEITH.

"If I can! *If I can!*" With a sudden movement of his hand the letter was put in one pocket, his watch taken out of another, and the button under the light pressed violently. It was eight - forty - five. The last train for Washington left at twelve-thirty, and a local from there reached Fredericksburg at nine-twenty-four the next morning. He knew the schedules well. "I have three hours and forty-five minutes," he said, under his breath. "I'd make it if there were but the forty-five minutes —if there were but ten."

126

A CHANGE OF PLANS

And then it was that Moses, coming in answer to the bell, concluded that his master was not himself. He had left him a few minutes before, unapproachable in his silence, unappreciative of his efforts to please and provide, and now he was giving so many orders at once, calling for this and for that, pulling out clothes and pushing them back, that Moses, who hated to be hurried as only his race can hate, stood helpless, knowing only that something had happened, something he did not understand.

"Did you say your riding-clothes, sir?" he asked, holding a dress-shirt in his hand. "Or did you say—"

"I don't know what I said." Laine knocked over a box of handkerchiefs and threw a white vest on the bed. "Where are my shaving things? I told you I didn't want a trunk. Take the durned thing away. I'll break my neck over it! Where is that English bag—the big one? Get it, will you, and put in my riding-clothes, evening clothes, and one other suit; put in the things I need. You've packed it often enough. Call up Jerdone's private number, and tell him I want all the flowers he's got. Get a move on you, Moses. If you're paralyzed tell me; if not—"

"No, sir. I ain't paralyzed. I just demoralizéd. Suddenness always did upset me. At dinner you look like you just as lief be dead as livin', and now—"

"You or I will be dead if I miss that twelve-thirty train. Have you called the cab?"

"No, sir. I ain't called no cab. You ain't never call the word cab. You mean—" Moses's hands dropped limply at his side. "You mean you're goin' away for Christmas?"

"That's what I mean!" Laine's voice was exultant, revealing, and he coughed to hide its ring. "By the way, Moses, why don't you go home for Christmas? Didn't you tell me once you came from Virginia? What part?"

"Palmyra, sir. In Fluvanna County, that's where I come from. Excuse me, but I bound to set down. Go *home?* Me go *home?* I couldn't git there and back not to save my life for lessen than twenty-five dollars, and till I git that farm paid for what I been buyin' to go back to and die on I can't go nowhere. That I can't."

Laine looked up from the collection of collars, cravats, and cuffs he was sorting. "Is it the money that's keeping you back, or is it you don't want to go?"

A CHANGE OF PLANS

"Don't want to go!" The palms of Moses's hands came together, opened, and came back. "Yesterday I near 'bout bus' open with wantin' to go. My mother she's near 'bout eighty, and she got Miss Lizzie to write me and beg me to come for this here Christmas. Miss Lizzie is old Major Pleasants's youngest old-maid daughter. He's got three of 'em. He was my mother's marster, old Major Pleasants was, and he sold me the land my mother's livin' on now. He didn't charge nothin' much for it, but I had to have a house built, and buy some pigs and some furniture and git a cow, and I bought two of them street-car mules what was in Richmond when they put the 'lectric cars on down there. 'T'was the first city in the United States to have 'em, Richmond was. They thought them mules was wore out, but there ain't no friskier ones in the county than they is, I tell you now. I ain't been home for four years—"

"And your mother is eighty?"

"Yes, sir, that's what they tell me, though she say she don't know herself 'ceptin' she had four chillern which was good size when the war broke out. I belong to the second crop. My mother done had nineteen chillern, the triflinest, good-for-nothin'est lot the Lord ever let live on this earth, if I do say it, and ain't a one of 'em what does a thing for her, savin' 'tis me and Eliza—Eliza she's my sister and lives with her."

"And you'd like to spend Christmas with your mother, you say?"

In the years of his service Moses had never before mentioned family matters, but, having started, he was not likely to stop, and Laine was forced to interrupt.

"Yes, sir. This Christmas I would. Some other Christmases I wouldn't, 'count of a yaller girl what lived on the next place. It was in the summer-time, the last time I was home, and, she bein' a likely-lookin' girl, I seen right much of her every now and then, and I just talk along and tell her 'bout New York and what a grand, lonely place it was, and how my heart got hongry for my own people, and—things like that, you know, but I didn't mean nothin' serious or have any matrimony ideas, and first thing I know she done had me engaged to her. She chase me near 'bout to death, that girl did, but Miss Lizzie say she gone away now and I can come in peace."

Laine took out his pocket-book, put some notes in an envelope, and handed it to Moses.

A CHANGE OF PLANS

"This is for your ticket and to get some things to take to your mother," he said. "Be back by the thirtieth, and hurry and call that cab for the twelve-thirty train. I've some letters to write before I leave, and there's no time to lose. Tell Caddie I want to see her, and don't forget about that Reilley family, and see that everything gets to them in good shape—a good dinner and all the bundles and plenty for the stockings. Tell Caddie I'm waiting."

Later on, in the library, Laine sealed his last letter and put it on the pile Moses was to mail in the morning. Perhaps he had been a little rash this Christmas. Well, suppose he had. The boys in the office had done well through the year and ought to be told so. By itself a check was a pretty cold thing, and the words he had written to each had been honestly meant. And Miss Dutton, his stenographer, needed a little trip. Ten days at Atlantic City with her mother would pull her up. She had been looking badly lately—worried about her mother, Weeks had told him. Pity she was so homely. It was pretty unfair the way women had to work at both ends of the line. Weeks, too, could get his wife that fur coat he'd been wanting her to have for three years. What an honest old duck Weeks was!—and who would ever believe him as full of sentiment as a boy of twenty? He had overheard him talking to Miss Dutton about the coat that morning. Fifteen years Weeks had been his secretary, but to-night was the first time he had ever told him in actual words of his appreciation of his faithful service. "I wouldn't want a million if it didn't have some love with it," Claudia had said to him, and before his half-closed eyes she seemed to stand in front of him.

"They are her gifts," he said. "I was blind, and she has made me see."

XVII

OT until he was settled in the car did Laine let himself take in the meaning of the journey he was taking. The past few hours had been too hurried to think; but as he sat in the smoking-compartment thought was no longer to be held in abeyance, and he yielded to it with no effort at restraint.

Sleep was impossible. The train, due at Washington at seven-twelve, would there have to be changed to a local for Fredericksburg, but the early rising was no hardship. To sit up all night would have been none. Each turn of the wheel was taking him nearer and nearer, and to listen to them was strange joy. Only that morning he had wished Christmas was over, had indeed counted the days before business could again absorb, and now every hour would be priceless, every moment to be held back hungrily.

133

fore answer could be made the driver was on the box, the whip was cracked, and two sleepy old horses began the slight incline of the long street out of which they presently turned to go to the wharf and the boat tied loosely to it.

Half an hour later, bags and boxes having been stored in a state-room, a hasty survey of the boat made, and a few words exchanged with a blue-coated man of friendly manners concerning the hour of departure, Laine again got in the old ramshackle hack and for two hours was shown the honors and glories of the little town which had hitherto been but a name and forever after was to be a smiling memory. Snow and slush covered its sidewalks, mud was deep in the middle of the streets, but the air went to the head with its stinging freshness, the sun shone brilliantly, and in the faces of the people was happy content.

Reins dropped loosely in his lap, Beauregarde, the driver, sat sideways on the box and emitted information in terms of his own; and Laine looked and listened in silent joy to statements made and the manner of their making.

"Yas, suh, this heah town am second only in historic con-se-quence to Williamsburg, suh, though folks don't know it till they come and

find it out from me.   I been a-drivin' this heah
hack and a-studyin' of history for more'n forty
years, and I ain't hardly scratch the skin of what
done happen heah before a Yankee man was
ever thought of.   They didn't use to have no
Yankees 'fore the war, but they done propogate
themselves so all over the land that they clean
got possession of 'most all of it.   They's worse
than them little English sparrows, they tell me.
Marse George Washington he used to walk
these streets on his way to school.   He had to
cross the river from Ferry Farm over yonder"
—the whip was waved vaguely in the air—"and
he wore long trousers till he got to be a man.
Young folks didn't use to show their legs in
those days, suh, jes' gentlemen.   That place
we're comin' to is Swan Tavern, and if it could
talk it could tell things that big men said, that
it could.   This heah house is where Mis' Mary,
the mother of Marse George Washington, used
to live when she got too old to boss the farm.
Some society owns it what was originated to
preserve our Virginia iniquities, and they done
put up a monument to her that's the onliest one
ever put up to a woman for being the mother of
a man.   They was bus head people, the
Washingtons was, but so was a lot of others who

didn't do nothin' to prove it, and so is now forgot, and quality folks in them days was so thick there warn't enough other kind to do 'em reverence. Governor Spottswood and his Horse-Shoe gentlemen took dinner once in this heah town, and President James Monroe used to live heah. I'm a-goin' to show you his home and his office, presently, and the house where Marse Paul Jones used to live in. I reckon you done heard tell of Marse John Paul Jones, ain't you?"

Laine admitted having heard of him, but historic personages did not interest as much as present-day ones. The occupants of certain quaint and charming old houses, with servants' quarters in the rear and flower-filled gardens in the front, the rose-bushes of which were now bent and burdened with snow, appealed, as the other places of famous associations failed to do, and he wondered in which of them Claudia's relatives lived.

At Marye's Heights Beauregarde waxed eloquent. Half of what he said was unheard, however, and as Laine's eyes swept the famous battle-fields his forehead wrinkled in fine folds. Could they have been settled in any other way—those questions which had torn a nation's heart from its bosom? Would the spilling of blood be forever necessary? He ordered Beauregarde to drive to the hotel. There was just time for lunch, and then the boat which would take him down the river to where Claudia would be waiting.

As the boat swung off from the wharf and slowly made its way down the narrow river, curving like a horse-shoe around its ice-bound banks, Laine, standing in the bow, scanned the scene closely, and wondered if it were but yesterday that he had been in the rush and stir of city life. Straight up from the water the bluff rose boldly. Rays of pale sunlight sent threads of rainbow colors on the snow which covered it, and through the crystal-coated trees, here and there, a stately mansion could be seen overlooking the river. Skimming the water, a sea-gull would now and then dip and splash and rise again in the clear, cold air, and, save for the throb of the engine, there was no sound.

Until the sun had set and darkness made farther scanning of banks and bluff and winding river impossible, Laine walked the deck, hands in pockets, and thought of the morrow and the days ahead. The boat would tie up for the night at Pratt's Wharf and was due at ten the next morning at Brooke Bank if there was no unusual delay. Suddenly he remembered she had said other friends would be on the boat. Most of the passengers were obviously returning home from a shopping trip to the city, package-laden and bundle-burdened, but two city men he had noticed and then forgotten in the thought of other things. Who were they? He opened the door of the stuffy little cabin and went in. Five minutes later he was at the supper-table and next to the two men who were talking in undertones of former Christmases at Elmwood. They were young, good-looking, and of Claudia's world. He got up and again went out.

XVIII

OR some time Laine had seen Claudia. Walking up and down the little wharf at the end of the long bridge, railless and narrow, which ran far out into the river, her hands in her muff, the collar of her fur coat turned up, her face unprotected by the brown veil which tied down securely the close-fitting hat, he had seen her a long way off, and as she waved her hand in greeting he lifted his hat and waved it in return.

A few minutes later he was shaking hands with her, with her uncle, with his two fellow-passengers, with a number of other people, and everybody was talking at once. Those on the wharf were calling out to those on the boat, and those on the boat were making inquiries of, or sending messages by those on the wharf, and not until Laine's hands were again shaken well

by Claudia's uncle as the *Essex* drew off, did
he understand just who was his host.

"A hearty welcome to Virginia, sir! A
hearty welcome! We're happy to have you in
our home! Here, Claudia, you drive Mr. Laine
in the small sleigh, and I'll take the boys in the
big one. Are you ready? Look at that rascal
Jim dancing a horn-pipe instead of filling that
wagon! We're glad to know you, sir, glad to
have you!" And for the third time Laine's
hands were shaken well by the ruddy-faced,
white-haired old gentleman, with the twinkling,
faded blue eyes, and old-fashioned clothes;
shaken until they hurt. He was no longer a
stranger. The touch of hands, the sound of
voice, and a something without name had made
him one of them, and that of which he had once
been doubtful he knew was true.

Ahead of them his fellow-travelers, one a
Keith cousin and the other a friend, waved back
and disappeared in a bend of the road; and as
Claudia took up the reins he turned toward her.

"Have you been waiting long? Are you sure
you are not cold?" he asked.

"Cold! On a day like this?" The color in
her face was brilliant. "We don't often have
weather of this sort, and to stay indoors is

impossible. I love it! It's so Christmasy, if it isn't Southern. Did you have a very dreadful trip down? It takes courage to make it."

"Courage!" He laughed and tucked the robe closer around her. "It was the most interesting trip I ever took. This is a very beautiful country."

"We think it is." She turned slightly and looked around her. The road from the boat-landing wound gradually up the incline to the ridge above the river; and as they reached its top the view of the latter was unbroken, and broad and blue it stretched between its snow-clad banks, serene and silent.

Laine's eyes swept the scene before him. The brilliant sunshine on field and river and winding road for a moment was blinding. The biting air stung his face, and life seemed suddenly a splendid, joyous thing. The girl beside him was looking ahead, as if at something to be seen there; and again he turned to her.

"You love it here?"

"Love it?" Her eyes were raised to his. "Everything in it, of it, about it!" With her left hand she brushed away the strands of hair the wind had blown across her eyes. "It is my home."

"A woman can make a home anywhere. A man—"

"No, she can't—that is, I couldn't. I'd smother in New York. It is wonderful to go to. I love its stir and color and the splendid things it is doing; but you can't listen to the wind in the trees, or watch the stars come out, or let your other self have a chance." She turned to him. "We're very slow and queer down here. Are you sure you won't mind coming for Christmas?"

Laine leaned forward and straightened the robe, and out of his face the color faded. He was only one of the several guests. "You are very good to let me come," he said, quietly. "I have not thanked you. I don't know how to thank you. Christmas by one's self—"

"Is unrighteous!" She nodded gaily and touched the horse with the whip. "There's Elmwood! There's my home! Please like Virginia, Mr. Vermont man!"

Before he could answer, the sleigh stopped at the entrance to the road leading to the big house, and at the door of the little lodge by the always-open gate stood a short, stout colored woman, hands on her hips, and on her head a gaily colored kerchief.

ELMWOOD

Laine was introduced. Mammy Malaprop was known by reputation, but no words could make of Malaprop a picture, and in deep delight Laine watched her as she curtsied in a manner all her own.

"How you do, suh! How you do! A superfluous Christmas to you, suh! I'm sorry you didn't git heah 'fore de war. Livin' nowadays ain't more'n shucks from de corn of what it used to be. Is dey all heah now, Miss Claudia?"

"I believe so. I am going to bring Mr. Laine down for some hoe-cakes and buttermilk after Christmas, and you might tell him some of the stories you used to tell us when we were children. He lives in New York, and—"

"He do! I hope he got himself petrified on the way down, for they tell me 'tis a den of promiscuity, and all the nations of the earth done took their seats in it. I knowed a woman who lived there once. She near 'bout work herself to death, and she say she couldn't have stood it if it hadn't been for the hopes of a glorious immorality what was awaitin' her when she died—" And Mammy Malaprop's hands waved cheerfully until the sleigh was lost to sight.

From the public road skirting the Elmwood land the private one, tree-bordered by century-old elms, leading to the terraced lawn, wound for some three-quarters of a mile, and as they approached the house Laine saw it was architecturally of a type unseen before. The central building, broad, two stories high, with sloping roof and deep-pillared portico, by itself would not have been unusual; but the slightly semicircular corridors connecting it with the two wings gave it a grace and beauty seldom found in the straight lines of the period in which it had been built, and the effect was impressive. At the foot of the terrace a little colored boy was blowing ardently a little trumpet, giving shrill greeting to the stranger guest, and as they came closer he took off his hat and held it in his hand.

"All right, Gabriel." Claudia nodded to the boy. "Run on, now, and tell Jeptha to come for the horse." She laughed in Laine's puzzled eyes. "He's Mammy Malaprop's grandson. He thinks he's the real Gabriel and it's his duty to blow. He sings like an angel, but can't learn to spell his name. There they are!" She waved her hand gaily to the group on the porch.

As he saw them Laine thought of Claudia's

arrival in New York, and his face flushed.
The men came down the steps, and a moment
later he was presented to Claudia's mother,
gracious, gentle, and of a dignity fine and sweet;
to her sister, home for the holidays with her
husband and children; to an engineer cousin
from the West, and a girl from Philadelphia;
and once more his hands were shaken by Colonel
Bushrod Ball. It was a Christmas guest who
was being welcomed, not Winthrop Laine alone,
and he wondered if he were indeed himself.

More than once he wondered before the day
was done. Under the leadership of the Colonel
the men were shown their rooms, by way of
the dining-room, for, like Moses, Uncle Bushrod believed inward cheer essential after out-
door chill; and, moreover, the apple toddy must
be tested. It was an old world he was in, but
to him a very new one. The happy stir of
Christmas preparations, the coming and going
of friends and neighbors, the informality and
absence of pretense, the gay chatter and genuine
interest, was warm and sweet; and as one who
watches a play he wondered at it, and something long thought dead thrilled and throbbed
and stirred within him.

In former days the house had doubtless been

the scene of lavish living, he thought from time to time, and he would have liked to explore the many rooms with their polished floors and deep window-seats, their carved paneling and marble mantels; and when, in the afternoon, he found himself alone for a few minutes in the vast hall, he paced off its sixty feet of length and its twenty of width to know their number, studied the winding staircase with its white pilasters and mahogany rails, scanned hurriedly the portraits in their tarnished frames, some with the signatures of Sir Joshua Reynolds, some with Stuart, and others of lesser fame, which hung above the wainscoted walls; and as he looked he did not wonder at Claudia's love for her home.

"You care for these things, too, do you?" The voice behind made him turn quickly. The girl from Philadelphia nodded to him and hugged her crossed arms closely to her bosom. "I don't. That is, not in weather like this, I don't. Ancestral halls sound well, but, unheated, they're horrors. I'm frozen, and the doors are open, of course. Have you been in the big parlors? Some pretty things are in them, but faded and rather shabby now. Why don't you go in the library? There's a

148

roaring fire in there, and a chair you can sit on. Every other one in the house has something in it."

Laine followed the girl into the library, and as she held her hands to the blaze she motioned him to sit down. "I don't believe anybody in the world is as crazy about Christmas as Claudia. She gets the whole county on the jump, and to-morrow night everything in it will be here. Giving is all right, but Claudia takes it too far. The house needs painting, and a furnace would make it a different place, but she will do nothing until she has the money in the bank to pay for it; and yet she will give everybody within miles a Christmas present. When she took hold of things the place was dreadfully mortgaged, and she's paid off every dollar; but, for chance, stock-markets aren't in it with farming. Isn't that a pretty old desk? I could sell lots of this furniture for them and get big money for it, but I don't dare say so. They never talk money here. My room hasn't a piece of carpet on it, and one of those old Joshua Reynoldses in the hall would get so many things the house needs. I'm a Philistine, I guess, as well as a Philadelphian, and I like new things: plenty of bath-rooms and electric lights and steam heat. I don't blame them for not selling the old silver and china or the dining-room furniture, though it needs doing over pretty badly; but some of those old peri-wigged pictures I'd sell in a minute. Plenty of people would pay well for ancestors, and it's about all they've got down here. Hello, Claudia; we were just talking about you!"

Claudia put down the armful of red roses she was carrying and began to fill a tall vase with them. "Did you say anything that wasn't nice?" She bit a piece of stem off. "If you did, it wasn't so." She turned to Laine. "You ought to see mother. She rarely has such flowers as you brought down— You have made her so happy. It was very good of you."

"Good!" The girl from Philadelphia went out of the room. "If only—" In his eyes no longer was restraint, and Claudia turned her head as if listening to something outside.

"I believe mother is calling me," she said. "Would you mind telling her, Mr. Laine, I am coming right away?"

XIX

LAINE looked at his watch. Twenty minutes past twelve. Christmas was over. Two days after were over also, and in the morning most of the guests were going away.

From the basket by the hearth he threw a fresh log on the smoldering fire, lifted it with his foot farther back on the hot ashes, drew the old-fashioned arm-chair closer to the fender, and, turning down the light from the lamp on the pie-crust table near the mantel, sat down and lighted a fresh cigar.

It had been very beautiful, very wonderful, this Christmas in the country. Its memories would go with him through life, and yet he must go away and say no word of what he had meant to say to Claudia.

Very definitely he had understood, from the day of his arrival, that to tell her of his love

151

would be a violation of a code to which the
directness of his nature had given little thought
in the reaction of feeling which had possessed
him when he read her note. He was a guest
by invitation, and to speak now would be beyond pardon. In his heart was no room for
humor, and yet a comic side of the situation
in which he found himself was undeniable.
The contrast it afforded to former opportuni-
ties was absurdly sharp and determined, and
the irony of the little god's way of doing things
was irritatingly manifest.

If in Claudia's heart was knowledge of the
secret in his, she masked it well. Warmly
cordial, coolly impersonal, frankly unconscious,
she had never avoided him, and still had so
managed that they were never alone together. Hands clasped loosely, he leaned forward and stared into the heart of the blazing
logs. Of course she knew. All women know
when they are loved. No. The log fell apart,
and its burning flame glowed rich and red.
She had not known, or she would not have
asked him to Elmwood. Merely as she would
ask any other lonely man in whom she felt a
kindly interest, she had asked him, and, thus
far, her home was the love of her life. In a

thousand ways he had felt it, seen it, understood it; and the man who would take her from it must awaken within her that which as yet was still asleep.

The days just past had been miserably happy. Before others light laughter and gay speech. In his heart surrender and suppliance, and before him always the necessity of silence until he could come again, and he must go that he might come again.

One by one, pictures of recent experiences passed before him, experiences of simple, happy, homelike living; and things he had almost forgotten to believe in seemed real and true once more. A new sense of values, a new understanding of the essentials of life, had been born again; and something growing cold and cynical had warmed and softened.

In the big hall he had helped the others put up the fragrant spruce pine-tree which reached to the ceiling, helped to dress it midst jolly chatter and joyous confusion, helped to hide the innumerable presents for the morrow's findings; and on Christmas morning had as eagerly dumped the contents of his stocking as had Jack and Janet, or the men who had come from busy city lives to be boys again, or as Claudia herself, who could not see with what her own was filled, for the constant demand that she should come here and there, and see this and that, or do what no one else was able to.

Slipping down farther in his chair, Laine put his feet on the fender and with half-shut eyes saw other pictures in the fire. The gray dawn of Christmas morning came again, and he seemed to hear the clear, childish voice below his window. Half asleep, he had stirred and wondered what it was, then sat up to listen. The quaint words of the old carols he knew well, but never had he heard them sung as Gabriel was singing them. Shrill and sweet in the crisp, cold air, the voice sounded first as if far away and then very near, and he knew the boy was walking up and down below each window that all might hear alike.

> As Joseph was a-walking
> He heard the angels sing,
> This night there shall be born
> Our heavenly King.

Here and there, in a verse from one carol joined almost in the same breath to another he went from:

CHRISTMAS

God rest you, merry gentlemen,
Let nothing you dismay.
Remember Christ, our Saviour,
Was born on Christmas Day.

to

We are not daily beggars,
That beg from door to door,
But we are neighbor's children
Whom you have seen before.

He had smiled at the mixture of verses and jumped up, for Jim had come in to light the fire, and from his broadly grinning face "Christmas Gif" was radiating, if from his lips, in obedience to orders, their utterance was withheld. On his door a half-hour later came the pounding of childish fists, and Janet's lisping voice was calling sturdily:

"Oh, Mither Laine, Santa Clauth hath come and your stocking ith down-stairs. Pleath, thir, hurry! Mother said I could kiss you a happy Chrithmath if you were drethed."

Hand in hand they had gone into the dining-room, with its lavishly spread table and mantel-hung stockings, and the chorus of hearty greetings and warm hand-shaking had made his heart beat like a boy's,

The day had passed quickly. The gay breakfast; the unwrapping of bundles; the sleigh-ride to church, where the service was not so long as was the seemingly social meeting afterward; the bountiful dinner with its table laden as in days of old rather than in the modern fashion of elegant emptiness; the short afternoon—it was all soon over, and the evening had gone even more rapidly.

The crackling logs and dancing flames in the huge old-fashioned fireplace in the hall, the tree with its myriad of lighted candles, the many guests from county's end to county's end, the delicious supper and foaming egg-nog, and, last of all, the Virginia reel danced in the vast parlors and led by Colonel Bushrod Ball and Madam Beverly, who had not missed a Christmas night at Elmwood since she was a bride some sixty years ago, made a memory to last through life, a memory more than beautiful if— He drew in a deep breath. There should be no "if."

Through the days and the evenings of the days that followed there had been no word alone with Claudia, however. She had taken him to see the Prossers, but Jack and Janet had gone with them, and out-of-doors and indoors there was always some one else. Was this done purposely?

He leaned forward and threw a couple of logs on the fire. The room was cold. As the wood caught and the flames curled around the rough bark, the big tester bed, with its carved posts and valance of white muslin, threw long shadows across the room, and in their brass candlesticks the candle-light flared fitfully from the mantel, touching lightly the bowl of holly with its scarlet berries, and throwing pale gleams of color on the polished panels of the old mahogany wardrobe on the opposite wall. For a moment he watched the play of fire and candle, then got up and began to walk backward and forward the length of the uncarpeted floor. Writing was a poor weapon with which to win a woman's heart. Rather would he tell her of his love, ask her to be his wife, and, if she would marry him, compel her to say when; but he could not come as quickly as he could write. He must go away that he might tell her what no longer was to be withheld. Indecision had ever been unendurable, and uncertainty was not in him to stand. Without her, life would be—again he looked in the fire— without her, life would not be life.

XX

CLAUDIA

CLAUDIA parted the curtains of her bedroom window and, holding them aside, looked out upon the scene before her with eyes love-filled at its wonder and beauty.

Across the broad, terraced lawn the fresh-fallen snow was unbroken, and every crystal-coated branch and twig of the great trees upon it gleamed in the moonlight as though made of glass. In the distance the river between its low hills seemed a shining, winding path of silver, and over it the moon hung white and clear and passionless. The mystery of silence, the majesty of things eternal, brooded softly; and with a sudden movement of her hands Claudia held them as though in prayer.

"In all the world there is no place like this —for me. It is my place. My work is here. I could not—could not!"

CLAUDIA

With a slight indrawing breath that was half sigh, half shiver, she left the window and drew her chair close to the fire. For a long time she looked into its dancing depths, and gradually her eyes so narrowed that their long lashes touched her flame-flushed cheeks. After a while she got up, went over to her desk, took from it several letters locked in a small drawer, came back to the fire, and again looked into it.

The girlish grace of her figure in its simple dress of soft blue, open at the neck and showing the curves of the beautiful throat, was emphasized by the unconscious relaxation of her body as she leaned for a moment against the mantel; and the Claudia to whom all looked for direction, the Claudia who had small patience with hesitating indecisions, and none for morbid self-questionings, searched the leaping flames with eyes uncertain and afraid.

A slight noise in the hall made her start uneasily. She did not want to be disturbed to-night. Turning her head, she listened. The corners of the large, high-ceilinged room, with its old-fashioned mahogany furniture, its shelves of books, its carved desk of quaint pattern, and its many touches of feminine occupancy, were lost in shadow, and only here and there on chair or table or bit of wall the firelight darted, but to dance off again, and the stillness was unbroken save by the crackling logs upon the hearth.

Drawing the lamp on the table closer, she sat down and took out of their opened envelopes two letters, one addressed to her mother and one to her Uncle Bushrod Ball; and as she read them the flush in her face deepened, then paled, and she bit her lip to hide its quivering. Putting them aside, she held for a moment, in hands that trembled slightly, another letter, and presently she began to read it:

"*December 30th.*

"I can wait no longer, Claudia. Words are not for love like mine; but you, who gave it life, will understand it without words. I believed I had put it from me—the thought of marriage—for almost I had lost my faith in the love for which I looked, and with compromise I could not be content. Perhaps I had no right to ask for what few find in life, but I did ask it, and when you came I knew my dreaming had come true. Will you marry me, Claudia? So infinitely I love you, want you, need you, that the days ahead until I win you

CLAUDIA

—for I shall win you—are dark and dreaded.
All of your love, its supremest best, I want;
but if for mine, which is beyond all measure,
you can give me now but little, give it and let
me come to you. I must come. I am coming.
And believe me always   Yours,
                    "WINTHROP LAINE."

The pages dropped slowly in her lap, and,
leaning back in her chair, Claudia closed her
eyes and pressed her hands against them
tightly. For some time she sat thus, then took
up the last letter and read that also.

                    "*December 31st.*
"It is within an hour of midnight, Claudia.
Soon the new year will be with us and the old
one gone—the one that brought you to me.
Almost the year had gone before I met you, but
time is more than days and weeks, and that of
ours together has been the real living of my
life. In the stillness of my room I drop my
book and dream that you are with me. On
the street I hurry home to you; and once I
stopped and bought you flowers—and in the
darkness threw them away. To have you
really here, to know that you are waiting—

161

"The new year has come, Claudia. The bells are striking the hour. It must, it shall bring you to me. I am asking much when I ask you to marry me, to leave your home to make a home for me. Your infinite love for Elmwood is understood well. Its old-world air of dignity and charm, of gracious courtesy and fine friendships, of proud memories and gentle peace, could scarce find counterpart elsewhere on earth, and yet in the days to come would it content alone, Claudia? For my great need of you might there not be some little need of me? Tell me I may come; but, whether you tell me or not, I am coming.

"WINTHROP LAINE."

Claudia put the pages back in their envelope. On the hearth the fire burned low, and, slipping out of her chair, she sat upon the rug and held her hands out shiveringly to the red ashes slowly turning gray. The habit of childhood was upon her, and quiveringly she talked to herself:

"You shouldn't have asked him to come Christmas! But how could I have known? I only thought he would be lonely. He cares for so few people and with all his wisdom has so little understanding of many things in life. He is so intolerant of weakness and meanness, of sham and show and pretence and make-believe that—that that's why you like him, and you know it, Claudia Keith! You shouldn't have asked him. You didn't know—but you knew before he went away. And he is coming back." Slowly she got up. "No. He is not coming back. That is, not yet, he isn't. You are not sure. Are you glad?" In the mirror over the mantel she met her eyes unshrinkingly. "Yes, I am glad," she said, and her lips whitened. "I am glad, but I am not sure." In her eyes was strange appeal. "Vermont and Virginia! Could we be happy? We are so different—and yet— Perhaps in the spring. . . . The winter months are very long. Oh, Winthrop Laine!" She pressed her hands to her heart as if to still its sudden throbbing, then reached for his letter and kissed it. "I wonder if I am going to know what Lonely Land can mean!"

XXI

A VISIT FROM DOROTHEA

DOROTHEA settled herself more comfortably in her uncle's lap. "You certainly ought to be thankful you've never had it," she said. "It's worse than being a leper. I've never been a leper, but when you're that you can go out, the Bible says so, and people just pass you by on the other side and let you alone. With diphtheria they don't let you alone. Lepers are just outcasts, but diphtherias—what are people who have diphtheria?—well, whatever they are, they're cast in and nobody can see them except the nurses and the doctor and your mother and father. The doctor said father mustn't come in my room, as he had to go to his business, and father told him to go to the devil—I heard him. I just love the way father talks when he's mad. I couldn't have stood the long days if it hadn't been for you and

164

father coming in every evening. They certainly do a lot of things when you're sick with contagiousness. Everything you eat out of and drink out of has to be boiled and stewed, and the things you spit in burned up, and the walls washed, and *more* foolishness!" Dorothea's eyes rolled and her voice was emphatic. "I don't believe in a lot of things, Uncle Winthrop. I wasn't really sick, and just had a teensy, weensy bit of pain in my throat; and if I'd known what they were going to do to me I'd have been one of those Science Christians and kept it to myself."

"But suppose you had given it to Channing?" Dorothea's uncle settled Dorothea more steadily on his lap. "The foolishness of wisdom is all some see of it, but if Channing had taken diphtheria from you—"

"I don't believe there was any diphtheria for him to take. If I'd been a poor person it would have been plain sore throat, and I'd had some peace. Timkins says his little girl was a heap sicker than I was, and her mother nursed her all the time, and she got well long before I did. Are we very rich, Uncle Winthrop?"

"You are not billionaires. Your father has been fortunate and made some money—"

THE MAN IN LONELY LAND

"I'll ask her." Dorothea slipped from her uncle's lap. "I'll be back in a minute," and before Laine could press the button which would bring Moses she had disappeared. Five minutes later she was back, in her hands a good-sized paper box, tied clumsily with red string, and as she put it on the table she patted it with satisfaction.

"That's for Channing," she said, half leaning against the table and drumming on it with the tips of her fingers. "Caddie didn't have any cakes. She says you used to like sweet things, and it was once a pleasure to cook for you; but if you enjoy anything you eat now you never confess it to her. She says you eat, but you don't know the name of what you're eating, and one thing is the same as another. I think her feelings are getting hurt, Uncle Winthrop."

"Are they? I'm sorry. Caddie is a spoiled creature. I long ago exhausted the English language in commendation of her efforts. Nothing is so wearing on one as continual demand for praise, and Caddie's capacity is exhaustless. I'm sorry she didn't have the little cakes."

"She's going to make some to-morrow and send them to me. It's pop-corn in this box."

A VISIT FROM DOROTHEA

Dorothea held up the latter and shook it. "Moses brought it from Virginia. They are the cunningest little ears you've ever saw. Wasn't it nice of Moses to think about us and bring it? Of course, he didn't know we would be away so long and that I was going to be sick and he wouldn't see me until spring; but it's a thing that keeps, and the drier it is the prettier it pops, he says. What is that picture over there, Uncle Winthrop? It is very ugly."

Laine glanced at the picture to which Dorothea pointed. "That is a Jan Steen — 'The Village Fair.' Sorry you don't like it. You think that Botticelli is ugly also. A little later in life it may meet with your approval. The original is priceless."

"A lot of priceless things aren't pretty. I don't ever expect to be a culturated person. Mother makes me go to all those old galleries and museums, when we're in Europe, and look at a lot of cracked pictures and broken statues and carved things, and wants me to think they're beautiful, but I don't. Some of them are hideous, and I get so tired of being told I must admire them that I make a face inside at most of them as I walk along, though, of course, outside, for mother's sake, I don't make any

12   169

signs. I'm a great disappointment to mother.
We had a lady artist guide the last time we
were in Italy. She used to get so mad with
me that once she shook me. Father would
have killed her if she hadn't been a lady, and
after that he and I used to go out by ourselves
and have the grandest times. He'd show me
just a few pictures at the time, and tell me all
about them, and some of them I just loved.
Mother says you have so many beautiful things,
Uncle Winthrop, and that it's a shame for a
man to have them all by himself." She looked
around the large room, and again took her seat
in her uncle's lap. "Some things I like in here,
and some I don't. You've got an awful lot of
books, haven't you?"

"Too many, I'm afraid. Would you mind if
I smoked?" Laine reached for a cigar from the
box on the table and held it between his fingers.
"May I?"

"Of course. I hope I won't forget, though,
and kiss you. I'm so apt to when I'm talking, if I like a person. Tobacco is so bitter.
I'll tell you what I think is the matter with
this room. It's—it's—" She looked around
carefully. "It's something that isn't in it. I
don't know what it is. Why don't you get

married, Uncle Winthrop? Maybe your wife would know."

Laine put the unlighted cigar back on the table, and Dorothea's hands, which were stroking one of his, were gripped by it and held tightly.

"I do not doubt it. The trouble is in getting the wife."

Dorothea sat upright. "The idea! I heard Miss Robin French say the other day the way unmarried men were run after was outrageous, and all they had to do was to stand still and crow a little, and up would come a-clucking all kinds of hens, little ones and big ones, and young ones and old ones, and— Don't you tell anybody, but I think she'd come, too!" Dorothea's hands came together, and she laughed gleefully. "Father says if Miss Robin would give up hoping she'd be happier." Suddenly her face sobered. "Do all ladies try to marry a man, Uncle Winthrop?"

"They most certainly do not." Laine smiled in Dorothea's face, and before the child's clear eyes his own, full of weary pain, turned away. "Many of them take very long to make up their minds to marry at all."

"Have you ever asked one to marry you?"

171

Laine did not answer. Dorothea's question was unheard. His thoughts were elsewhere.

"Have you?"

"Have I what?"

"Ever asked a lady to marry you?"

"I have."

The hand which Dorothea had been stroking was dropped. She sprang to her feet and stood in front of him, her hands clasped in rigid excitement on her breast.

"When"—her voice curled upward in quivering delight—"when is she going to do it, Uncle Winthrop?"

"I do not know. She has not said she would do it at all."

"Not said—she would—marry—*you!*" Delight had changed to indignation high and shrill, and Dorothea's eyes blazed brilliantly. "Is she a crazy lady?"

"She is not."

"Then why?"

"She is not quite sure she— It is not a thing to talk about, Dorothea." He drew her again on his lap and unclasped the clenched fingers. "We are good friends, you and I, and I have told you what I have told no one else. So far as I am concerned, it does not matter who knows, but until she decides we will not talk of this again. You understand, don't you, Dorothea?"

"I understand she must have very little sense. I don't see how you could want to marry a lady who didn't know right off, the very first minute, that she wanted to marry you. Do—do I know her, Uncle Winthrop?"

"You do."

For a moment there was silence, broken only by the ticking of the clock on the mantel; and slowly Dorothea turned to her uncle, her big brown eyes troubled and uncertain. For half a moment she looked at him, then, without warning, threw her arms around his neck and hid her face against his.

"Is—is—it Claudia, Uncle Winthrop?" she whispered. "Is—it—my cousin Claudia?"

"It is—your cousin Claudia."

The quiver in Laine's voice was beyond control, and, lifting the child's face, he kissed it. "I have asked her to marry me, Dorothea, but not yet has she promised to do so."

In Dorothea's cheeks two burning spots of red glowed brilliantly. Slipping down from her uncle's lap, she drew a long breath. "I knew she must be queer about something," she

173

said, and her fingers interlocked in trembling excitement. "She was too nice not to be, but I didn't think she'd be this kind of queer. The idea of not promising right away! I know what's the matter. It's her home and her mother, and all the things she is doing in the country that she don't want to give up. Why don't you go down there and make her, Uncle Winthrop?"

"She asks me not to come—yet. There is no hotel, and—"

"Does she write to you?"

Laine smiled in the eager eyes. "Yes, she writes to me."

Again there was silence, and presently a queer sound from Dorothea. "I can't help it, Uncle Winthrop! They're coming! Won't it be grand, because she will, I know she will, and I'm so glad I can't—can't help—" And big, happy tears rolled down Dorothea's face, which was pressed close to Laine's as he held her close to his heart.

That night, when all the house was still and every one asleep, Dorothea slipped out of bed and, kneeling down beside it, folded her hands and began to pray.

"O Lord"—her voice was a high whisper—

174

A VISIT FROM DOROTHEA

"please make my cousin Claudia come to her senses and promise my uncle Winthrop that she will marry him right away. She lives in Virginia. Her post-office is Brooke Bank, and she's an awfully nice person, but father says even You don't know why women do like they do sometimes, and of course a man don't. Please make her love him so hard she'd just die without him, and make her write him to come quick. Give her plenteous sense from on high, and fill her with heavenly thankfulness and make her my aunt for ever and ever. Amen."

She got up and scrambled into bed and closed her eyes tightly. "French prayers aren't worth a cent when you want something and want it quick," she said, half aloud. "And when you're in dead earnest you have to get right down on your knees. I don't know what I'd do if I couldn't talk in plain English to the Lord. I hope He will answer, for if He don't I certainly couldn't say right off, 'Thy will be done.' I'd say I thought my cousin Claudia had mighty little sense."

XXII

SPRINGTIME

INTHROP LAINE lifted the tangled vines which overhung the shrub-bordered path leading down the sloping lawn at the back of the house to the rose-garden at its foot, and held them so that Claudia could pass under.

"They ought to be cut." She stopped and unfastened a long tendril of intertwined honeysuckle and bridal-wreath which had caught her hair. "Everything ought to be cut and fixed, only—"

"It would be beyond pardon. If any one should attempt to change this garden, death should be the penalty. One rarely sees such old-fashioned flowers as are here, never in modern places."

"No one knows when many of them were planted, and nothing hurts them." Stooping,

SPRINGTIME

Claudia picked from the ground a few violets and lilies-of-the-valley growing around the trunk of an immense elm-tree at the end of the path, then looked up.

"Don't let's go to the roses yet. I want to see what the sun-dial says. This is the way my great-grandmother used to come to meet my great-grandfather when she was a girl. Her parents wanted her to marry some one else. She would slip out of the house and down this path to that big magnolia-tree, from where she could see and not be seen, and it was there they made their plans to run away."

"We will go there. It looks like a very nice place at which to make plans."

Into Claudia's face color sprang quickly, and for a moment she drew back. "Oh no! It is too beautiful to-day to make plans of any kind. It is enough to just—live. You haven't seen half of Elmwood yet, and you want to talk of—other things."

"I certainly do." Laine stepped back that Claudia might lead the way down the path, box-bordered so high that those within could not be seen outside, and smiled in the protesting face. A few moments more and they had come out to the front lawn on the left of the house

177

and some distance below the terrace on which
it overlooked the river, and as they reached a
group of spreading magnolias he drew in his
breath.

"I do not wonder that you love it. And I
am asking you to leave it!"

She looked up. "Come, I want to show you
some of the old things, the dear things, and
then—"

"We will come back, and you will tell me
what I must know, Claudia?"

She nodded and pulled the bells from the
lily-of-the-valley she held in her hands. "We
will come back and—I will tell you."

For an hour, in the soft glow of the sun now
sinking in the heavens, they wandered through
the grounds and separate gardens of the old
estate, now walking the length of the long
avenue, shaded by great elms of more than
century age, now around the lawn with its
beds of bleeding-hearts and snowdrops, of
wall-flowers and sweet-William, of hyacinths
and tulips, with their borders of violets and
cowslips, of candytuft and verbenas, and . at
the old sun-dial they stopped and read the
hour. Picking an armful of lilacs and cali-
canthus and snowballs and blue flags, planted

in the days when the great trees were tiny sap-
lings, they sent them in by Gabriel, who was
following at a distance, blowing softly on his
trumpet, and for some minutes stood in front
of the house and watched the sun touch, here
and there, the old brick laid in Flemish bond;
then went back and sat down on the low seat
under the big magnolia, from which the river
could be glimpsed, and over which every now
and then a white sail could be seen.

Behind them the sun sank. The mass of
shifting gold and blue and crimson and pale
purple lost little by little its brilliant splendor,
and slowly over land and sky soft twilight fell,
and only here and there was heard the song
and twitter of birds as they made ready for
the night.

For a few moments there was silence, and
then in his Laine held the hands of Claudia.

"It is a wonder world, this old, old world
of yours with its many things we have forgotten. And yet—you will come to me? You
are sure at last, Claudia?"

"I am sure—at last." She raised her eyes
to his. "I could not let you come until I
knew that—all the homes in all the world
would not be home without—"

"Without what, Claudia?"

"Without— Why do you make me tell you when you know? You make me tell too much."

"You cannot tell too much. Claudia! Claudia!"

Overhead the birds chirped sleepily and one by one the stars came out. Presently Claudia drew herself away and smoothed her kissed and wind-blown hair. "I am such a queer person. I think you ought to know," she said, and again her shining eyes were raised to his. "There are a great many things I don't care for, and I don't think the way some people do about a good many other things. I had to take long to be sure."

"It was very cruel, Claudia." He lifted her face to his and smiled in the confessing eyes. "My forgiveness proves the measure of my love. As proof of penitence, will you marry me in June?"

"I certainly—will—not!" Again she drew away. "Jacqueline will not get here until July. I told you she was coming home to live. You don't suppose I'd leave my mother before Jacqueline comes home?"

SPRINGTIME

"Then when?"

"In October, perhaps." Slowly the color crept to her temples. "It is so beautiful here in October. There isn't a month in all the year it will not hurt to leave." Sudden tears were in her eyes. "But it would hurt worse not to be—with—you. They were very long, Winthrop, the winter months that followed Christmas. You have very poor manners. You should have written first and told me you had enjoyed yourself instead of telling—"

"What I could no longer keep back? There was no time for manners. I had to know."

"But you didn't, and because I couldn't tell you. Before, I have always been so quick to know. To go away—with just you! I had to be so certain there was no other way of happiness." In the darkness she shivered slightly, and Laine drew her into his arms and held her close.

"Perhaps"—her voice was so low he had to bend his head to hear it—"perhaps it is because we are apart from the things that make one forget that I have thought more about what it should mean—what marriage should mean—than I might have done had there been no time to think. It is forever, Winthrop, this life that we are entering. Are we very, very sure there's love enough to last?"

"I am very sure, Claudia." He lifted her hands to his lips and kissed them. "For me your love will make of life a—"

"Land that is not lonely?" Under her breath she laughed, to hide the sob in her throat. "Oh, Winthrop Laine, it is what love is for! And no one's land is lonely when there is love enough!"

THE END